by
Greg Jones Ellis

STEELE SPRING
STAGE RIGHTS
www.stagerights.com

DIVINITY PLACE

For all stage performance inquiries, please contact:

Steele Spring Stage Rights
3845 Cazador Street
Los Angeles, CA 90065
(323) 739-0413
www.stagerights.com

PRODUCTION HISTORY

An earlier version of *Divinity Place,* entitled *On Divinity,* has had staged readings at HBO's Screening Room in New York (sponsored by the New York chapter of the National Academy of Television Arts and Sciences), the Newman Center for the Performing Arts (in the Elizabeth Eriksen Byron Theatre) at the University of Denver and the Hartt School at the University of Hartford.

CAST OF CHARACTERS

7F, 4M

JEAN (Regina McManus): F, 24. The bride to be. Hides her nerves with either hysterical laughter or slightly salty language.

CAPUTO (Angela Caputo Provenzano): F, 24. Jean's wisecracking best friend. Very pregnant.

NICKI (Ludmila Wisnicki Scarzy): F, 24. Deadpan friend of Jean.

MARGUERITE McManus: F, 27. Jean's sister. Single and not happy about it. Tries to be the boss to Jean and Fixie, but is generally regarded as just butting in.

CEIL (Cecilia O'Connell): F, 30. Jean and Marguerite's cousin and owner of the house. Warm, loving, motherly, but a demon when it comes to keeping a clean house.

JINX (Genevieve Kelly): F, 26. Future sister-in-law to Jean and Marguerite. Chubby and the "odd man out" among the young women. Doesn't get humor and is easily offended.

BUDDY Sinclair: M, 24. Jean's fiancé. Wholesome, open, and fun-loving.

FIXIE (Francis Xavier McManus): M, 26. Jinx's fiancé, Jean and Marguerite's brother, Buddy's best friend. Clumsy, sweet.

FATHER BRENDAN: M, 30+. Local priest. Soft-spoken, earnest.

HOLY JOE (Monsignor Aloysius McDonough): M, 50+. Parish pastor. Strikes fear in the hearts of his parishioners.

MRS. SINCLAIR: F, 50+. Buddy's mother. Lives under the thumb of her husband.

MR. SINCLAIR: M, 50+. Buddy's father. Irascible, tyrannical, and a match for Holy Joe.

SETTING

1942: The parlor of a Row House in West Philadelphia.

SET NOTES

The suggested arrangement of the set are that there be a solid door leading to the front stoop up right and a swinging door to the kitchen stage right. These can be reversed if wing space dictates. A staircase upstage is needed. It may be helpful to place the sofa (for the love scene in Act II) further downstage than other set pieces.

RUN TIME

90 Minutes

AUTHOR'S NOTES

It may be surprising to learn that much of this play is based on true events in the lives of the playwright's parents. The setting— indeed, the title of the play— really exists: a row house in Philadelphia on Divinity Place. West Philadelphia, like many neighborhoods in large American cities, defined itself in the mid-20th century largely by the ethnic makeup of its inhabitants. Many neighborhoods still do. While the play takes place in the 1940s, it is meant to show something we all still grapple with: territoriality and ignorance slumber under the surface of neighborly peace, until an event like a wedding wakes up the sleeping ogres. It can create a little farce like this play, or it can tear the world apart. But lessons are best learned with laughter. The main objective for the creative team behind a production of this play should be to celebrate the triumph of love.

1. Both "In the Shade of the Old Apple Tree" and "Those Wedding Bells Are Breaking up That Old Gang of Mine" are real songs. The melodies are easily obtained by looking the songs up on the internet. The parody lyrics to "In the Shade of the Old Apple Tree" are not the original, and bear no copyright. The lyrics to "Those Wedding Bells Are Breaking up That Old Gang of Mine" are the original. These are intended to be sung as if by amateurs like the characters that sing them. No attempt to "stage" them as "numbers" should be made.

2. Towards the end of Act I Scene 1, the actor playing Ceil is invited to come up with as much comic business in cleaning the house as she and the director choose. The result should be a marvel of both efficiency and panic that is intended to be a silent, comic tour de force.

3. Jean's laughter has to be both funny and increasingly inappropriate so that the other characters react accordingly.

4. In order to make Jinx's dress fall apart on cue, the dress should be held together with anything that doesn't either make noise (so no Velcro) or hurt the actor playing Jinx (pins). The best bet might be snaps sown at strategic places. The actor playing Jinx should then rehearse how to time it so she is pulling off a snap before that particular piece of the dress "falls" off.

AUTHOR'S NOTES (CONT'D)

5. While the women on whom this is based truly spoke with this kind of slang, profanity, and mild irreverence toward their priests and nuns, make sure that they all remain innocents in the eyes of the audience. Unlike today, each time they make a naughty remark, there should be a sense that they would never talk like this in front of the elder generation. And remember, every unmarried character in the play is completely inexperienced when it comes to sex!

6. The Philadelphia accent as used by these characters during this time period is fast disappearing. However, it is quite distinctive from other regional accents of the Eastern Seaboard. If you feel that your cast or audience may be too unfamiliar with this, the accent should be avoided. If you attempt it, you will want to pay particular attention to the word "sister" as it applies to the name of a nun. In this time and place, it would be pronounced "stir." Additionally, the term "out the home" is correctly written here. It is similar to the expression "down the shore," as used by people on the East Coast near Philadelphia. Finally, when Holy Joe tells the young people to "find a seat and light there," this is also correct as written. It is a regionalism meant to mean "alight" (as a bird finds a perch and "alights" there).

ACT I

SCENE 1

In darkness, we hear a young woman's voice (CAPUTO) sing the following:

CAPUTO'S VOICE:
IN THE SHADE OF THE OLD APPLE TREE,
SAT TWO IRISHMEN DRUNK AS CAN BE,

> *The stage is still dark. CAPUTO's voice is joined by that of JEAN, NIKKI and MARGUERITE. The three sing:*

CAPUTO, JEAN, NIKKI & MARGUERITE'S VOICES:
SAID PAT TO HIS FRIEND,
"THERE'S A FLY ON THE END
OF MY NOSE, WON'T YOU CHASE IT FOR ME?"

> *The lights are now up, revealing the parlor of 1330 Divinity Place. It is a typical row house in Philadelphia, circa August 1942. The singers are revealed to be SIX WOMEN, meeting for their monthly Friday night "club"— an excuse to get together and let their men— if they have them— do the same elsewhere.*
>
> *CAPUTO, who started the singing in a broad, barrelhouse style, is very pregnant. Her best friend JEAN, their pal NICKI, and Jean's sister MARGUERITE, sit near her. They are now hesitantly joined by CEIL, the older cousin of Jean and Marguerite and the head of the household here on Divinity Place. They all sing:*

ALL BUT JINX:
NOW MIKE WAS A REGULAR GUY
SO HE PICKED UP THE AXE THAT LAY BY
AND HE LAID THAT FLY FLAT,
AND THEY BURIED POOR PAT
IN THE SHADE OF THE OLD APPLE TREE!

> *JINX, a plump little persimmon, who is engaged to Fixie (Jean and Marguerite's brother), has definitely not joined in, although she is very much present. All but Jinx finish the song, followed by good-natured laughter.*
>
> *The GIRLS are obviously having a good time, but it is 9:30, and it's almost time to break up— this is 1942.*
>
> *And JEAN is having trouble sitting still.*

JEAN (*still laughing*): Oh, God, Caputo, did you and I catch hell from Sister Euphemia for that one!

CAPUTO: How the hell did I know her real name used to be Colleen Dougherty?

MARGUERITE (*laughing, but with an edge*): Yeah, and you two got away without a lecture.

JEAN: Poor Marguerite. Hey, Caputo and I got kitchen duty for a month.

MARGUERITE: Serves you right. You shoulda known better than to sing that within earshot of the sisters. At least half of them have the map of Ireland on their pusses.

JINX: Hey, don't make fun of us Irish.

MARGUERITE: We can always make fun of our own. Caputo can kid the dagos, can't she?

CAPUTO (*earnestly*): Of course.

JEAN: And, Nicki, what are you again?

NICKI: Thirsty.

> *She drains the last of her drink.*
>
> *Laughter. During all this, CEIL is picking up glasses, wiping rings on the furniture, etc.*

JEAN: No, I always forget— I keep thinking you're Polish, but you're not, right?

MARGUERITE: Nope, she's a Polack. Right, Nicki?

NICKI: Latvian, actually.

CAPUTO: Latvian? What's that?

NICKI: Lithuanian, only better.

> *Silence. Nobody really knows what that means.*

MARGUERITE: But Catholic, anyway.

NICKI: I'm not sure.

MARGUERITE: What?

NICKI: Originally, I mean. My grandmother sent me out the home after my mother died.

CEIL: Well, wasn't she Catholic?

NICKI: I don't know. (*Pause*) Jeez, I am— is that ok?

> *After due consideration, they shrug and move on.*

MARGUERITE: Mr. Kachevski out the home was Polish, though, right?

CAPUTO: God, I forgot all about him! (*To Jinx and Ceil*) He did the fix-it stuff around the grounds. Yeah. (*She starts to laugh again*) I remember him. He didn't speak-a de English so good. This one (*Points to Jean*) sent him downtown to the hardware store for a bucket of elbow grease!

General laughter.

JEAN: Ah, he was such a nice guy. But, I just couldn't resist.

MARGUERITE: That's your problem— no self-control.

JEAN: God, you sound just like them.

MARGUERITE: Who?

JEAN: The penguins. Gosh, Mr. Kachevski could fix anything, couldn't he?

MARGUERITE: How would you know?

JEAN: I'm engaged to the world's greatest mechanic, aren't I?

CAPUTO: Oh, yeah? How's he handle his tools?

Shocked laughter by most— not CEIL or JINX.

JINX: I don't get it.

More whoops of laughter.

JEAN: Oh, God. My poor brother. Sounds like he's not going to get it either.

Laughs.

MARGUERITE: Don't worry, Jinx— we'll explain it all to you both before your wedding.

JINX *(warming to the topic)*: I can hardly wait. Ma has the dress pattern all cut out. She pinned me into it last night.

CAPUTO *(sotto voce to Nicki)*: Pin shortage hits Philly.

JINX *(continuing)*: We've got the veil from my grandmother and the shoes. And my Dad is already practicing walking me down the aisle. *(To Jean and Marguerite, with too much sympathy)* I just wish your parents could be there.

JEAN: Well, they'll be watching.

JINX: I thank God every day my mother and father are alive to see me get married. I don't know what I'd do if I lost them. You girls are very impressive. Being able to joke about a place like...

CAPUTO *(flaring)*: A place like what?

JINX: I don't know how I could face it.

CAPUTO: You'd get along.

JEAN: Look. Our parents died. Nobody else wanted us. We could have been split up; we could have been hired out. Instead, we had three meals a day, a high school education. I had a ball.

NICKI: And most of the nuns were swell.

CAPUTO: Except Euphie.

JEAN: Ah, Euphie could be a good egg. Remember when I took the sled out at night and gashed up my leg? She ran me all the way downtown in the middle of the night to have it stitched up.

MARGUERITE: And called me into her office the next day to tell me to look after you better! We weren't even in the same dormitory— what was I supposed to do, run a bed check at two in the morning?

JEAN: Poor Marguerite.

MARGUERITE: Yeah, poor Marguerite. And now, when I go back to help at the card parties, all the nuns come up and ask me, "How's Jean?" I feel like telling them, "Oh, she's just the same. Headed for hell."

CEIL *(interrupting)*: I'll make the coffee. The boys'll be here soon.

CAPUTO: Ah, come on, Ceil. Have a highball. We'll help you clean up, honest. Here, there's just enough left.

> *She picks up a pint bottle of whiskey, which sits next to a bottle of ginger ale, both nearly empty.*

CEIL: Don't you have another one!

CAPUTO: I only had one. I've been drinking ginger ale all night.

CEIL: Well, you shouldn't have had even one. You don't want to bring a little drunkard into the world.

> *She exits to the kitchen, right.*

MARGUERITE *(reaching for the bottle)*: I'll finish it up.

> *JEAN and CAPUTO look at each other meaningfully.*

CAPUTO: What's Ceil so bent out of shape about?

JEAN *(with affection)*: She was just born worried.

MARGUERITE: God knows she's had enough to worry about.

JEAN: Will you get off my back?

MARGUERITE: What'd I say?

JEAN: I meant that Ceil's had her share.

MARGUERITE: So did I!

CAPUTO: Whoa! Sisters! Round one over!

JEAN *(begins to giggle)*: Sorry. I'm just a little keyed up.

NICKI: Uh-oh. What's up?

> *JEAN giggles even more.*

CAPUTO: Jeez. This has gotta be big.

> *JEAN's giggles prevent her from talking.*

NICKI: Let me guess. You joined the WACs.

CAPUTO: Are you kidding? Look at her. She's too pretty for the WACs.

JINX: Hey, my cousin Bernadette's going into the WACs.

CAPUTO: Exactly.

NICKI: Well, you can't be going into the convent. Not with somebody like Buddy sniffing around you.

MARGUERITE: What's wrong with the convent?

CAPUTO: Oh, here we go.

MARGUERITE: Don't make fun. I may take the veil myself.

General hooting from CAPUTO, NICKI and JEAN.

It's...

The GIRLS all finish the rest of the sentence, each with her own take on it.

ALL: —the greatest thing a girl can do.

CAPUTO *(back to Jean)*: Well, you don't look pregnant. I know about pregnant.

JEAN *(collecting herself, with a purposeful look, stands up)*: Everybody take a little ginger ale.

She pours a little in each one's glass.

Just a little. We're having a toast. *(Calling)* Ceil, come back in here!

MARGUERITE: Let me make a toast.

JEAN: Nope. This is a special toast.

NICKI: This does sound good. So fancy with her toasts.

CEIL enters. JEAN gives her a glass.

CEIL: No, now I said I don't want a highball. I'm making coffee—

JEAN: No, it's just ginger ale. Take it. *(She takes a deep breath)* Well... here's to my last night as Jean McManus.

They all look confused. Long pause...

CAPUTO *(finally catching on)*: You don't mean—

JEAN *(blurting it out)*: Buddy and I are getting married. Tomorrow.

ALL: Tomorrow!?

*General hubbub. *All together:*

*MARGUERITE: You've got to be kidding!

*NICKI: How 'bout that!

*CAPUTO: You dirty stinker! How could you keep this from your best pal?

*CEIL: Oh, my! Oh, oh! My! my!

JINX just sits in silence.

CAPUTO: Jeez, I could pop the baby out right here! You devil! What's up? Couldn't wait until the wedding night, huh?

JEAN: No. Well... if you want to know the truth... well, that is part of it.

MARGUERITE: Regina Agnes McManus!

JEAN: And the fact that Buddy's getting ready to join up—

EVERYONE: What?

JEAN: It's only a matter of time. And I don't want to see him off without... well, without being his wife. It's time.

MARGUERITE: But you've only been engaged since Christmas.

JEAN: And it's August, for crying' out loud.

NICKI: I think it's sweet. Stan and I knew the minute we said "June" that we'd never hold out that long. And look what happened. He's reporting for his physical next week.

JEAN: That's right. So you did the only thing you could do. You moved it up a few months.

NICKI: Of course that wasn't easy. What with rearranging everything. And with Grandma and everybody. But she adjusted... more or less... eventually.

CEIL: How is your grandmother?

NICKI: Oh, much better since the wedding. Another week and the doctor says she can come downstairs for a whole day.

JEAN *(getting back to proving her own point)*: But you're happy.

NICKI *(deadpan)*: Oh, God, yeah.

> *Everybody waits for her to elaborate. She doesn't.*

MARGUERITE: This is impossible. We could not possibly get everybody together on such short notice. Plus, they'd all think you had to get married, no matter what you said.

JEAN: So, let 'em.

> *CAPUTO and NICKI laugh. The others don't find it funny.*

And exactly who do we have to notify, the society page at the Bulletin?

MARGUERITE: The family.

JEAN: What family? Everybody I want is here. Right here at 1330 Divinity Place. My wonderful cousin Ceil. My wonderful brother Fixie. *(To Caputo and Nicki)* My wonderful fellow survivors of St. Vincent's. *(To Marguerite)* And you.

MARGUERITE: The aunts— Aunt Rae, Aunt Kate... *(Significantly)* Aunt Mary.

JEAN: They don't really want to come. They'd have to cough up a present. You know how tight the old girls are.

MARGUERITE: Aunt Mary is our guardian, for God's sake. You couldn't leave her out.

JEAN *(quietly)*: I don't want her there.

MARGUERITE: Why?

CEIL: Jean, you have to have your Aunt Mary. She took care of you when your Mama died.

JEAN: No, she didn't! She put us out the home!

JINX: I thought you liked the home.

JEAN: I did. But it's not like Aunt Mary raised us. Sister *(Pronounced "Stir")* Bernadine, Sister Mary Alice, Sister Euphemia— they raised us. She just wrote the checks.

CEIL *(kindly)*: Jeannie. It would be like you not wanting me there. You really do want me there, don't you?

JEAN *(melting)*: Of course I really want you there. My God, you're not just my cousin, for God's sake. You took Marguerite and me in after graduation. You gave us our start. You keep us all on the square. You're family.

MARGUERITE: So is Aunt Mary. Handling Mother and Father's money after they died couldn't have been easy.

JEAN: She's a bookkeeper, Marguerite. It's what she does for a living. She just added us to her books.

NICKI: Maybe I am the dumb Polack after all. Tell me again— why does it have to be tomorrow?

JEAN: Well, we talked about it. Buddy's sure he's gonna be drafted sooner or later. He's just trying to set up his garage. *(Smiling)* We really don't want to wait much more. *(Pause)* And... well, if we gave everybody enough notice, we're afraid they'd spend all their time talking us out of it.

CAPUTO: Bingo. The shoe drops. His parents don't know.

JEAN: No. It's the goofiest thing. They know we're engaged. But they just don't think we'll ever get married. At least his father doesn't.

CEIL: What about your Aunt Mary? What did she say last December?

JEAN: Nothing.

MARGUERITE: You told her, didn't you?

JEAN: No.

MARGUERITE: I can't believe you! After all that woman did for you!

JEAN: I swear, if you didn't live in this house, I wouldn't have told you.

NICKI: What about your dress?

JEAN *(warming to the topic)*: I bought a new grey suit— wait'll you see it!

> CEIL starts to go into panic mode, her usual state when
> things get too spontaneous for her taste.

CEIL: My Lord, what about the priest? What about the church? What about the lunch?

JEAN: We got Father Brendan to do it. He's been really great about it. Only... we can't get married in the church, so he finagled it so he can marry us here tomorrow... if that's alright, Ceil.

CEIL: Can you get married in a house?

JEAN *(somewhat ruefully)*: You can if the groom isn't Catholic.

CAPUTO *(winking)*: Is it legal?

JEAN: I hope so. And I want you to be my matron of honor.

CAPUTO *(pleased)*: God, what can I wear? I don't have any dressy tents.

> *Looks around the room, spies an armchair with a big, obvious slipcover. She yanks it off the chair, puts it around herself, and throws a lace doily from a table over her chest.*

Wait. Now I'm ready.

> *Laughter.*

JEAN *(reluctantly)*: And, Marguerite, you're my sister. So, if you keep your mouth shut, you can be my maid of honor.

MARGUERITE *(feigning surprise)*: Oh! I never would have thought... I never would have hoped...

CAPUTO *(sarcastically)*: You never would have let us hear the end of it if she didn't.

JEAN: Ceil, Nicki... I wish I could have you as something...

NICKI: How 'bout flower girl?

> *They all laugh.*

CEIL: Don't be silly. I'll be too tired to be anything.

JEAN: What do you mean?

CEIL: I have to get this place ready. It'll take all night. Excuse me, girls. I have to find the silver polish.

> *She goes into the kitchen.*

> *Suddenly everyone seems to realize that JINX hasn't said anything.*

JEAN: Oh. Jinx. Buddy's asking Fixie to be his best man. Won't that be nice?

> *JINX purses her lips.*

And... you'll be the... best man's fiancée! And my sister-in-law!

> *The lips get tighter.*

> *(To everyone)*

Buddy's with Fixie right now. He's been with Father Brendan taking the last night of instruction. Oh, not real instruction, but, you know, in order to marry a Catholic. Buddy says he hasn't learned a damn thing about Catholics, but Father Brendan's such a Phillies fan he knows the batting average of every guy on the team!

> *They laugh.*

It's all kinda silly, really, his having to learn about my religion. I don't have to learn about his. Not that there's all that much to learn, from the way he tells it.

JEAN (CONT'D): "You go to church on Sunday, you treat people the way you want to be treated, and you don't sleep with anybody 'til you get married." I told him, "Shit, Catholics believe the same thing! Only in Latin!"

They all— but JINX— have a good laugh.

NICKI: I like Father Brendan. He's very down to earth.

CAPUTO: For a priest.

NICKI: You know what I mean, Angie. He's a regular guy.

JEAN: And he's young. I think that's why Buddy agreed to see him. At first my Boy Scout wasn't too keen on this whole thing, but he and Father Brendan hit it off right away.

JINX is still pursed. And saying nothing— loud and clear.

(After noticing Jinx)

And, we've gotten the blood test, the license, the works. Everything's all set. Girls, I'm sorry I've been so secretive. I don't know, I just didn't want to queer anything at the last minute. Does that make sense?

CAPUTO: Sure it does, kid.

MARGUERITE: I'm calling Aunt Mary.

JEAN: Oh, no you're not!

MARGUERITE: I'm going down to the druggie and I'm calling her up!

She heads for the door.

JEAN *(blocking her way)*: You do and you can both find yourselves locked out on the porch come tomorrow morning!

MARGUERITE: She's the closest thing you've got to a mother!

JEAN: She's the closest thing I've got to a boil on my behind! She was mean to mother, she was mean to us... when did she come out and see us? When she had to buy us new uniforms and wasn't sure how much we'd grown. Where was she when we started our periods?

MARGUERITE *(disgusted)*: Oh. Ooh!

JEAN: Where was she when we needed bras? When we started shaving our legs?

MARGUERITE: Leave it to you to put your head in the gutter.

JEAN: I did the right thing. I took Buddy to meet her. She put on a sour puss and barely talked to him. The sweetest guy in the world. Apparently the only thing that stuck in her stewpot head was that Buddy fixed cars. Who'd she call when her precious Packard broke down all the way up in Germantown? Buddy.

MARGUERITE *(after a long pause, mutters)*: Selfish.

JEAN: Yeah, I'm selfish. That's me. Listen, Buddy and I have enough people trying to grab happiness away from us. His father hates me. Aunt Mary hates him. And Hitler hates everybody. You're coming close to joining that bunch, do you hear? Now either you let me have one happy day all my way, or you can kiss— me goodbye. (Pause, turning to Jinx, steamed up) And what the hell is your problem?

JINX (getting up): I'll see if Ceil needs help polishing the silver.

> Exits quickly. The girls look at each other, baffled at Jinx's behavior.
>
> The front door opens. In bounds BUDDY, who immediately runs to the center of the room and stands on his head. He is followed by Francis Xavier McManus, better known as FIXIE. Bespectacled and good-natured, he dutifully closes the door after them and ambles over to his SISTERS, kissing them each on the cheek.

FIXIE: Where's Jinx?

CAPUTO: Off to join the foreign legion.

NICKI: She's in the kitchen helping Ceil with the silver.

CAPUTO: And from the looks of things, you'd better stop her before she melts it all down into one big, fat knife.

FIXIE: Huh?

JEAN, MARGUERITE, CAPUTO & NICKI (together): In the kitchen.

> FIXIE exits to the kitchen.

BUDDY (still upside down, looks at Nicki's legs): Hey, Nicki, your seams are crooked.

> They all laugh. NICKI checks her seams.

JEAN: Come here, clown. Kiss me.

BUDDY (snapping to his feet in one movement): Yes, Captain.

> They kiss, warmly and long. The GIRLS react by humming "Here Comes the Bride" through their noses.

BUDDY: Uh oh. (Imitating a radio newsman) "There's good news tonight, Mr. and Mrs. America." (To Jean) You told them, huh?

JEAN: Wasn't that the plan?

BUDDY: Yep. (To Caputo and Nicki) We told the boys. Uh... I think they'll be there tomorrow.

CAPUTO: They really tied one on?

BUDDY (sheepishly): Yeah.

JEAN: How was Father Brendan?

BUDDY: Great! Tonight he taught me who looks good for the pennant. It ain't the Phillies. Actually, he's taught me a lot since I've been meeting with him.

JEAN: Like what?

BUDDY: Like why a bunt isn't such a great idea most of the time. Did you know that most bunts end in multiple outs?

JEAN: No. You see, Catholics are smarter than Protestants.

BUDDY: So you say. He didn't know Babe Ruth's lifetime batting average.

CAPUTO: Is Babe Ruth Catholic?

BUDDY: I don't think so.

CAPUTO: That's why. Come to think of it, even if he was, priests wouldn't know much about him until after he was canonized.

BUDDY: What's canonized?

MARGUERITE, NICKI, CAPUTO & JEAN *(in unison)*: Made a saint.

CAPUTO: Once you're a saint, though, the priests know every time you took a crap.

NICKI: Yeah, and if they saved any of it, it becomes a relic.

The GIRLS crack up.

JEAN: Is Father all set for tomorrow?

BUDDY: All set. He said old Monsignor's not too choked up with him, but he's not forbidding it. Is that good?

CAPUTO: With Old Holy Joe? That's practically a blessing. You mean he took his tongue out of the beer keg long enough to say a sentence?

NICKI: Angie! That's too much.

CAPUTO: Oh, come on, you know as well as I do...

JEAN: Yeah, but it's not nice to make fun. God knows most of us know about drunks. It's not that funny.

CAPUTO: That's it for the jokes, folks.

JEAN *(to Buddy)*: Do you have everything?

BUDDY: You mean everything I was born with?

There's an oh-so-brief moment of innocent, but palpable, lust between the two.

JEAN: Stop. I mean, do you have everything we need to... do it.

The GIRLS hoot. BUDDY looks sheepish but devilish. JEAN doesn't know what she's said.

JEAN: What?

The other GIRLS suddenly scream with laughter.

CAPUTO: Yeah, Buddy. Did Father Brendan give you any instructions about that?

JEAN *(good-naturedly)*: What'd I say?

BUDDY: Never mind, honey. I have... everything we need.

> *The GIRLS are off again.*

To get married.

JEAN: That's what I said! I swear, one highball and they're off to the races!

> *FIXIE and JINX enter. Jinx is still pouting.*

FIXIE: Come on, Shug. How can I answer if you won't tell me what's wrong?

CAPUTO: Are her garters still in a crimp? Jinx, what is with you?

JINX *(dramatically, as if delivering the Word of God)*: As if you didn't know.

JEAN: We don't know!

JINX: I knew you didn't want me in your club. I know you hate me. *(She waits for denials, they do not come)* But I never knew you'd plot to ruin my whole life!

> *She breaks into an incredibly annoying bawl.*

NICKI: What did we do?

JINX *(through sobs)*: Oh, ho, ho! Very funny!

CAPUTO *(dryly)*: Well, I'm hysterical.

JEAN *(gently goes to her, puts her arms around her)*: Jinx, sweetie... what do you think we did to you?

JINX: My own sister-in-law-to-be!

FIXIE *(to Jean)*: What did you do to her?

JEAN: Oh, shut up. How the hell should I know? We were having some laughs, I told them Buddy and I were getting married tomorrow and the next thing you know –

> *A wail from JINX.*

JEAN: What? What?

JINX: What about my wedding?

JEAN: What about it?

JINX: I wanted to go first.

> *More sobs.*

JEAN: Go where?

JINX: Down... the... aisle!!

> *Thunderous tears. It finally hits everyone.*

FIXIE: Hey, that's right! You weren't supposed to get married 'til two weeks after us!

CAPUTO: Oh, for crying out loud, Fixie, this isn't England. This is 1942, for God's sake. America.

FIXIE: It's not right. We should get married in order.

MARGUERITE: Well, seeing as I'm the oldest, somebody better find me a man by midnight or the whole thing's loused up!

FIXIE: I meant... oh, you know what I mean.

JINX: You'll steal all my thunder! You'll make me look like yesterday's news.

FIXIE: And, as your older brother, I absolutely forbid it!

JEAN: Oh you do, do you?

FIXIE *(apprehensively)*: Yeah.

> *JEAN slowly advances toward FIXIE and looks him intensely in the eye, then pushes him down with a super shove and begins wrestling ferociously with him. After a brief struggle, she pins him and, still holding him down, says:*

Listen, you. Buddy and I are getting married tomorrow. In this living room. I'll be in a new suit and so will Buddy. Our wedding will be followed by whatever Ceil can get from the butter and egg man with what's left of the week's kitty. There's no veil, no bouquet, no music and no presents.

> *FIXIE struggles to get up. She repins him and continues:*

You and the pride of the Mummers here will have a church wedding and high Mass, with flowers and organ and prayer books and presents and a gown and a tux. All courtesy of Jinx's family, who are going into hock so you two can have what she wants. If you think that our little tap dance is gonna outshine Jinx's Ziegfeld Follies, then... that's your tough luck!

> *She almost lets him up, but then thinks better of it.*

Did Buddy ask you to be best man?

FIXIE *(quietly)*: Yes.

JEAN: What'd you say?

FIXIE: Well, that was before I thought about it...

JEAN *(pins him hard)*: What'd you say?

FIXIE: I said yes.

JEAN: Well, if you still feel that way, speak now or forever hold your peace.

> *FIXIE strains around hard to try and look at JINX.*

FIXIE: Honey?

JINX *(the lips are pursed again)*: Make up your own mind.

> *FIXIE, torn between two very determined women— and pinned to the floor by one of them— is in torture.*

BUDDY: Let him up, Jean.

JEAN: Huh?

BUDDY: Come on, no guy should have to make a decision with his sister's knees cutting off his windpipe. Let him up, honey.

Reluctantly, she does.

Francis, my pal, don't worry about it. I asked you to be my best man before the women got involved. When it was just two men, two friends. And your Irish eyes were smilin' for me. I'll understand if you have to say no, now.

BUDDY offers FIXIE his hand. Fixie slowly shakes it. Still clasping Buddy's hand, Fixie turns to JINX.

FIXIE: Sweetie... we'll still have the biggest wedding money can buy.

JINX *(not taking defeat well, bursts into tears again)*: Fine with me, Francis Xavier McManus. Side with your sister and your best friend. I'm only going to be your wife!

She storms out the front door.

FIXIE: Jinxie!

He runs to the door after her, stops, remembering something, turns to JEAN.

My good suit! It's still dirty from last week's Mass. I fell down the steps, remember?

JEAN: I had it cleaned Wednesday. It's hanging in your closet.

FIXIE: I... I guess I'll see you tomorrow. Right now, I gotta—

BUDDY: We know, pal. See you in the morning. Ten sharp!

FIXIE, distraught and confused, nods, bumps into the doorjamb, and beats an awkward retreat out the door.

CAPUTO: Boy! Is he in for one helluva marriage.

NICKI: I think she'll be good for him. Give him a little gumption.

MARGUERITE: I think she's a pain in the ass. But, who am I? I'm just the big sister. *(Looking at her watch)* And it's ten o'clock. You girls have two hours to find me a husband. As long as he's rich and Catholic.

CAPUTO: In that order, of course. *(To Nicki)* Well, come on, Polack, or whatever you are. I guess the boys went home without checking where their baggage was. We better get home before they start looking for us in the bawdyhouses. *(Goes over to Jean, gives her a hug)* I think it's swell. But you sure as hell don't give a girl any notice. Hey, and don't you worry— my cousin Sal runs a flower shop. I'll be here at nine thirty tomorrow with a bouquet, corsage for Marguerite and me and boutonnieres for the boys. That is, if I'm not at Misericordia Hospital givin' birth to little Mario here.

MARGUERITE *(alarmed)*: You're not ready yet, are you?

CAPUTO: Nah. Only seven months.

MARGUERITE: Are you sure? You're pretty big.

CAPUTO: Thanks. That's what the doctor says, anyway. How should I know? Like Jean says, it's not like we learned a lot from the nuns on that score. Nah, I'm alright. I just meant from all the excitement this one here's giving us...

NICKI: You'll be alright. *(To Jean)* Hey, kid, how'd you like to wear my veil? I'd offer you my gown, but you're a little... bustier than me.

JEAN: Thanks. Listen... I'm really sorry I didn't tell you sooner.

CAPUTO: Don't be silly.

NICKI: See you tomorrow, kid.

JEAN: Be careful getting to the trolley.

BUDDY *(springing to his feet)*: I'll give you a lift on my motorcycle.

CAPUTO: That's all right. I'd like the little bambino to stay there for awhile.

BUDDY: I'll walk youse, then.

CAPUTO: Nope. We're fine. Stay here and try for second base.

JEAN: He got there months ago.

NICKI: Attaboy.

JEAN: Ange?

CAPUTO: Yeah?

JEAN: Could Sal spare a corsage for Ceil?

CAPUTO: You betcha. 'Night, Marguerite.

MARGUERITE: 'Night. 'Night, Nicki.

NICKI: 'Night.

                    NICKI and CAPUTO exit.

MARGUERITE: Well, why don't we sit down with a nightcap and talk over tomorrow's festivities?

BUDDY *(simultaneously)*: Okay.

JEAN *(simultaneously)*: No.

MARGUERITE: Buddy, you want a beer or a highball?

BUDDY: Neither.

JEAN: He doesn't drink, remember? He's Presbyterian. And I thought all the booze was gone.

MARGUERITE *(removes a bottle from the sideboard, fixing herself a drink)*: All the company booze. I knew a Presbyterian who drank.

BUDDY: Oh, we can. I just don't.

MARGUERITE: I guess I never have seen you take a drink, have I? Or have I?

BUDDY: Nope.

JEAN: Can we get on with this? What do you need to know?

MARGUERITE *(ignoring her, to Buddy)*: I would like to invite our legal guardian to the wedding. As it is, I'll wake her up if I call now. But, before it gets any later, I'd like your permission to invite her.

JEAN: I told you—

MARGUERITE: I'm asking the man for his permission. Buddy?

BUDDY *(pause, thinking long and hard, then, to Jean)*: What do you think, honey?

JEAN: She knows what I think. She just doesn't care! She wants to invite Aunt Mary and nothing will stop her until she does!

MARGUERITE *(calmly, to Buddy)*: I just thought that it was only right that the woman who has looked out for our welfare be invited to her niece's wedding. To share in the joy, just as your parents will...

BUDDY: My parents won't be coming.

MARGUERITE: Why not?

BUDDY: My mother would like to come, but my father won't let her. *(To Jean)* She slipped me twenty bucks and said to tell you she's so sorry.

MARGUERITE: Maybe this should tell you two something. You can't be married in the church; your parents don't want to come...

JEAN: You just heard him say his mother—

MARGUERITE: You don't want your family there. Maybe this is all a little hasty.

JEAN: We've been going together four years! And he's our brother's best friend, for Christ's sake! Hasty, my foot!

> CEIL rushes in from the kitchen with a bucket on her arm. She has put a duster on to protect her clothes, and maybe even rubber gloves. And a scarf. During the next exchanges until Ceil exits, the following takes place: Ceil drops to the floor in one swoop, rolling up the rug with determination and awesome skill, lifting end tables, tipping sofas and chairs, all the while rolling the carpet as she goes. When she's finished baring the floor, she slaps down a soapy scrubbing brush and begins scrubbing. At first, the remaining trio observes with mute awe, but eventually MARGUERITE breaks the spell. But Ceil goes on.

MARGUERITE: Ceil, Jean doesn't want to invite Aunt Mary.

CEIL *(never looking up from her work)*: Uh-huh.

MARGUERITE: Ceil, she doesn't want to invite the head of our family.

CEIL: Your family, you mean. I'm from your mother's side.

MARGUERITE: What I mean is, she's not inviting the most important person to the wedding.

CEIL: Honey, the most important person you want to show up at your wedding is the person who said he'd be your husband. Second is the priest. And you have to have two people stand up for you. Everybody else is just lace trimming. Be glad you were invited. *(She suddenly has a thought)* Blessed sakes, I don't have enough coffee. Marguerite, will you run over to Cousin Sheila's and ask if you can borrow a pound until Monday? Oh— Jean, is Sheila invited?

JEAN: No.

CEIL *(a pause)*: Good. Nobody can stand her anyway. Alright. Marguerite, see if you can borrow some from Mrs. Sinclair instead.

MARGUERITE: Mrs. Sinclair? *(Points to Buddy)* She's his mother, why doesn't he go?

CEIL: Because once he's in the house, she'll want him to stay there. His father's due to get off his trolley shift, and I think these two would like few minutes.

MARGUERITE: Oh, alright. You can borrow coffee from her, but she won't come to your wedding.

BUDDY: Can't.

MARGUERITE: Crazy world.

> She exits.

CEIL: True enough. *(She stands up and surveys all she still needs to accomplish, wearily)* Alright, you two. You've got five minutes. Get your— er, talking in quick. I don't want Mr. Sinclair banging at my door again, asking for his wayward son. Lord God, the time he came down, scared the life out of me! I thought God himself was at my door! *(To Buddy)* And you hiding on the second floor landing. So make it quick. I don't want the soap to dry on my floor!

> She goes into the kitchen, mentally doing inventory as she exits.

JEAN: Well.

BUDDY: Well.

JEAN: So, you know all about us Catholics, now, huh?

BUDDY: You know, I really did read all the pamphlets from Holy Joe. Father Brendan said he had to give them to me. I'm glad he did. *(Teasing)* I want to know all about you and your kind!

JEAN: Oh, our kind, huh?

BUDDY: I want to know what you believe, and what makes you believe. All the holidays, the saints. It's really fascinating.

JEAN: Try having it drilled into you every day for twelve years.

BUDDY: But don't you find it beautiful?

JEAN: Yeah. I guess. I love the stories. Bernadette. St. Theresa.

BUDDY: And you seem to have an answer for every question.

JEAN: Who, me?

BUDDY (laughs): Like your catechism. All those deep, deep questions! And the longest answer in the whole thing only takes up about three lines. "Who made you?" "God made me." "Why did God make you—

JEAN: Yeah, yeah. Did Father Brendan have you memorize that stuff?

BUDDY: No. I guess it just stuck in my mind. It's all so simple. But not simple like silly. Simple to grasp, to... hold onto.

JEAN: Watch it, there. Looks like you want to convert after all. If you do, I'm supposed to rush you to a priest before you cool down.

BUDDY (smiles): No. I don't believe all of it. But I... appreciate it more. I, I actually enjoyed reading it! Besides, it's the only part that wasn't in Latin!

> CEIL sticks her head out of the kitchen.

CEIL: Stop jabbering! You've got two minutes!

> She disappears.

> JEAN and BUDDY suddenly realize this is their last moment together, alone, until the wedding. They kiss, with passion, sadness, maybe even a little panic. They come up for air... then kiss again.

> Suddenly, MARGUERITE flies in the door.

MARGUERITE: Mother of God, get outta here! Your father's trolley just pulled in.

JEAN: Did you get the coffee?

MARGUERITE: Get him outta here!

BUDDY: You know, my father's not that—

CEIL (popping her head in again): Get out!!

BUDDY (to Jean): See you tomorrow, I guess.

JEAN: I guess.

MARGUERITE & CEIL: Out!!

> BUDDY exits.

> Seeing her floor, she comes in, drops, and resumes cleaning.

CEIL: Jesus, Mary and St. Joseph.

> Note: Every time someone says "Jesus," every Catholic in the room does a quick head bow— and so, JEAN, MARGUERITE and CEIL do so— Ceil a bit belatedly.

> (To Marguerite)

Did you get the coffee?

MARGUERITE: She only had enough for Mr. Sinclair's breakfast.

CEIL *(gazing heavenward)*: Do you have to test me, dear God? Isn't coffee rationing enough? *(To Jean)* How much do you hate Cousin Sheila?

JEAN: I'll go door to door tomorrow until I scare up some coffee. *(Laughs, affectionately)* You could worry a dog to death.

CEIL: I just want... if you could've given me enough time, I—

                        She begins to tear up.

JEAN *(goes over to comfort her)*: Ceil— you have done everything for me. Some day I promise, we'll fix you a wedding, and you don't have to tell us until ten minutes before!

CEIL *(laughs ruefully)*: I probably won't know until ten minutes before, either!

MARGUERITE: Ceil and I will be just fine. There are plenty of fish in the sea. And if not, we'll just grow old together here, like Aunt Rae and Aunt Kate.

CEIL *(considers this, then, briskly changing the subject)*: Now, let's go over everything before you go to bed.

JEAN: What about you?

CEIL: Good Lord, no! I'll be up all night! That's what I needed all that coffee for! I have half a pound, but that'll be gone by the time everyone gets here! *(Sees the floor)* Oh, dear God, it's drying! *(She hits the deck and begins scrubbing again)* Jean, just say "yes" or "no." Dress?

JEAN: Yep, the grey suit. Wait'll you—

CEIL: Clean and pressed?

JEAN: Yes.

CEIL: Veil?

JEAN: I'm wearing Nicki's.

CEIL: Shoes?

JEAN: Yes.

CEIL: Polished?

JEAN: Yes.

CEIL: Bra?

JEAN: Yes.

CEIL: Other... things?

MARGUERITE *(pouring the last of another highball for herself)*: Boy, that's a neat way of wrapping up the list.

CEIL: I mean... lingerie, stockings, garters...

JEAN: Yes.

CEIL: Makeup?

JEAN: Yes.

The lights slowly fade as CEIL scrubs, JEAN helps clean up, and MARGUERITE yawns.

CEIL: Toilet water?

JEAN: Yes.

CEIL: Jewelry?

JEAN *(laughs)*: Does my miraculous medal count?

Blackout.

SCENE 2

SATURDAY, 9:00 A.M.

The front door opens slowly. MARGUERITE tiptoes in. She is wearing a sedate little dress and a lace mantilla on her head. She starts walking behind the sofa toward the stairs. As she heads up the stairs, CEIL, clad in a bathrobe and arms filled with dirty clothes, bounds down the stairs running right into Marguerite. They both scream.

CEIL: Lord, you scared me to death! What time is it?

MARGUERITE: Nine o'clock.

CEIL *(noting Marguerite's outfit)*: Did you go to church?

Snatching off her mantilla. JEAN comes down the stairs. ALL THREE WOMEN are standing on various levels of the steps.

MARGUERITE: I was lighting a candle for Jean's happiness.

CEIL *(suspiciously)*: What else were you doing?

JEAN: Did you call Aunt Mary?

MARGUERITE: No. *(Then she crosses herself, to God)* Forgive me, dear God. *(To Jean)* Alright, I tried to. She wasn't home.

JEAN: Marguerite, I told you—

MARGUERITE: I know! I felt bad so I stopped off at the church and prayed for your soul. And I made a confession.

CEIL *(looking around at what still needs to be done, to Marguerite)*: Go bring in the broom, will you, hon?

MARGUERITE: I'm all dressed up!

CEIL: Please?

MARGUERITE: Oh, all right.

She exits to kitchen.

CEIL: Be nice to your sister. She's not showing it, but I think she's a little upset with all this.

JEAN: It's not my fault—

CEIL: I know, sweetie. But it's not easy seeing your sister get married.

JEAN *(suddenly aware, gently)*: Ceil. You seemed so happy when Annie got married.

CEIL *(proudly)*: And wasn't I, then?

JEAN: I'm sorry. I didn't mean—

CEIL *(softening)*: You know, I loved taking over everything when Poppa died. I run this house. I raised the rest of the kids. And I loved it. God forgive me, but I did.

JEAN: You were only 16. You were a kid yourself.

CEIL *(remembering)*: Annie 12 and Katie... never going to grow up right.

JEAN: Poor Katie.

CEIL: My Katie's in heaven with our parents. Bless her.

JEAN: You know, you'll be rid of Marguerite and me soon. Then it'll be your turn to have some fun.

> *Hugs CEIL.*

CEIL *(laughs quietly)*: Won't that be a time? *(Calling to kitchen)* Marguerite! The broom!

MARGUERITE *(entering with the broom)*: I'm coming!

JEAN *(to Ceil)*: You poor slob. You been up all night. Why don't you go up and take a nice bath?

CEIL: But...

JEAN: The house is as clean as it's going to be. You could amputate a leg on the dining room table, it's so clean.

> *CEIL reluctantly heads upstairs.*

CEIL: Make sure you give a final sweep, now. The dust has finally settled.

MARGUERITE: Somehow I doubt that.

> *She casually starts sweeping anyway. JEAN finds a newspaper and uses it as a dustpan every time MARGUERITE sweeps a little pile of dust. She empties the little bit of dust into an ashtray.*

JEAN: I'm sorry I've been so short with you.

MARGUERITE: It's okay. And I'm sorry I tried to call Aunt Mary.

JEAN: And I'm sorry if I hurt your feelings

MARGUERITE: About what?

JEAN: Never mind. Listen... be nice to Ceil when I'm gone.

MARGUERITE: What do you mean? I'm nice to her.

JEAN *(laughs ironically)*: OK. I'm not going to argue with you. Just remember, you try bossing her around like you did Fixie and me, and you could be out on your ass.

MARGUERITE: Ceil wouldn't do that. We're blood.

JEAN: Yeah, and if you think blood's thicker than water, wait'll she punches you in the nose. Ceil isn't your slave.

MARGUERITE: You're just being spiteful.

JEAN: Skip it. Did you really pray for me this morning?

MARGUERITE: Of course I did. You need all the help you can get. Plus, *(Looks heavenward)* I had a talk with Mother.

JEAN: Here we go...

MARGUERITE: I don't care what you say. Mother would expect me, as the oldest, to... see to everything. *(Petulantly)* But you two won't let me!!

JEAN *(dryly)*: What'd Mother say?

MARGUERITE: Don't be smart. I just felt that I needed to let her know about everything, and... ask her a few things.

JEAN: Well, what'd she say?

MARGUERITE: Never mind!!! I just feel better, that's all.

JEAN: Well, good.

MARGUERITE: I just wish you were marrying a Catholic—

JEAN: Ohhh!!!

MARGUERITE *(conciliatory)*: But... I know you were just the unfortunate victim of circumstance.

JEAN: What circumstance?

MARGUERITE *(rolling her eyes)*: The time we all went to Midnight Mass! Buddy came with Fixie to see what it was all about. And you thought you saw the divine look of conversion in his eyes. And it was only the look of shock— Holy Joe had set his sleeve on fire with the censer.

JEAN: Boy! You're wiftier than I thought! "The divine look of conversion!" That's your routine, not mine.

MARGUERITE: What then?

JEAN: What— why I fell in love with Buddy? I don't know... lots of things. He didn't kid around like other boys. He... he kinda takes a minute to size up whether you'll like what he's about to say— whether it would offend you, or annoy you, or make you look at him as if to say, "What's so funny?" And his eyes have this soft haze, a sort of half-shy, half-mischievous, half-curious—

MARGUERITE: That's too many halves.

JEAN: —shut up— look of fun. As if to say, "I hope that made your day. Did it? 'Cause if it didn't, I'll make up for it, I swear." Ooh, I'm lightheaded just talking about it. And conviction. He's not a fool. He knows what he wants, and he knows the difference between right and wrong. How many men can you say that about?

MARGUERITE: Father Brendan, Holy Joe, all the priests I've met...

JEAN: I mean men, Marguerite. The kind you can kiss— with your tongue!

MARGUERITE: Uggh! That's it. That's absolutely the most disgusting thing you've ever said.

> *By now, the place is swept and MARGUERITE heads for the kitchen with the broom and the ashtray.*

JEAN: God help us.

MARGUERITE: God help you.

> *There is a knock at the door. MARGUERITE puts down the broom and reflexively heads for the door.*

With that filth on your mind, you're going to need all the prayers offered up for you. *(As she opens the door, her face still toward Jean)* Honestly! "Kiss a man with your tongue!" *(She sees, in horror that, it is...)* Father Brendan! *(Marguerite stands in abject horror)* Uh— Uh—

JEAN: Good morning, Father! You're early! That's good, I guess— means you're not chickening out!

> *FATHER BRENDAN, a thirtyish priest with a friendly air and, at present, a heavy heart, enters.*

FATHER BRENDAN: Good morning, Jean.

JEAN *(sensing something)*: What's up, Father?

FATHER BRENDAN: Oh, Jean, I'm so sorry.

JEAN *(with real fear)*: What? Is it Buddy? What, Father?

FATHER BRENDAN: I'm sure he's fine. No, I'm sure he's busy getting ready for the wedding. I came to you first because... well, I guess because you're the Catholic.

JEAN: Father, you're scaring me. What is it?

FATHER BRENDAN: I... won't be marrying you.

JEAN & MARGUERITE: What?

FATHER BRENDAN: Monsignor will be officiating.

JEAN: Holy Joe?

FATHER BRENDAN: I'm afraid so.

JEAN: But why? You're the one who's been giving Buddy instructions. You're the one who agreed to perform the wedding here on Divinity Place instead of the rectory. What made you change your mind?

FATHER BRENDAN: Oh, nothing. But Holy J— Monsignor McDonough— had a change of heart. He says he wants a chance to talk to both of you before the wedding.

JEAN *(to Marguerite)*: Who heard your confession this morning?

MARGUERITE *(sheepishly)*: Holy Joe, but—

JEAN: God DAMN it! Sorry, Father, but— oh, God DAMN it, Marguerite!

MARGUERITE: I didn't SAY anything! I just said I wanted to make sure I wasn't supposed to do anything more to... to persuade you to...

JEAN: If you queered this thing, I swear, I'll—

FATHER BRENDAN: No, no. He told me he's willing to perform the ceremony. I think. I'm so confused. He told me I have to go over to the shipyard and... bless some cargo.

JEAN: What cargo?

FATHER BRENDAN: I don't know. I guess with all the... U-boats and whatnot, the cargo needs all the help it can get.

JEAN: Can't Holy Joe bless the cargo?

FATHER BRENDAN: I guess not. I'm truly sorry, Jean. Give my best to Buddy, will you? And may Our Lord bless your union.

JEAN: Bless it? I hope he lets it happen...

FATHER BRENDAN: So do I. Well, I better get to the shipyard. Again... so sorry.

> *He exits.*

JEAN *(fighting the urge to cry— and also mad as hell)*: Shit!

> *CEIL comes down the stairs.*

CEIL: Who was that at the door? Did Sheila bring the coffee?

JEAN: Shit, shit, shit!! The wedding's off!

CEIL: What?

JEAN *(pointing to Marguerite)*: This one told Holy Joe it was a bad idea!

MARGUERITE: I did not!! I just thought he should have a talk with you!

JEAN: That's it! You're out of the wedding, if it ever takes place, thanks to you!

CEIL: What happened?

JEAN: This one told Holy Joe, and Holy Joe sent Father Brendan off to bless some shit bound for Europe, and Holy Joe's coming over here to talk me out of getting married, and he won't perform the ceremony. And I'll die without—

CEIL: Now, maybe he just wants to make sure it's all... official.

JEAN: Are you taking her side?

CEIL: I'm not taking anyone's side. Calm down.

JEAN: I don't want to calm down.

CEIL: Where's Fixie? He'll talk to you.

JEAN: He's off picking up that cow he calls a fiancée.

CEIL: Jean! Now that's enough! Be quiet before you call me something horrible! I just couldn't stand for that to happen.

JEAN *(softening)*: Oh, God. What's the matter with me? So what if Holy Joe marries us? He will marry us, don't you think?

CEIL: I hope so.

JEAN *(gazing heavenward)*: Dear God, Holy Mother Mary, and St. Anthony, please forgive me. I went to confession yesterday, as you know. And I said three extra acts of contrition just because I want to come into this marriage clean. Please, please let it go off without a hitch. Let Buddy's father not know until we're halfway through Delaware on our honeymoon. Let Buddy's mother live after she tells his father. And let me get through the honeymoon without getting my period.

CEIL *(simultaneously)*: Jean!

MARGUERITE *(simultaneously)*: Regina!

JEAN: If you can't do it all, then please, please just let us get married today. Let us have one hour of pure peace and I promise I'll put up with whatever shit you have waiting for us. Amen. *(To Ceil)* Now, I'm going up to finish getting ready. *(To Marguerite)* Would you like to help me?

MARGUERITE: O-Okay.

JEAN: Okay.

> *They go upstairs*

CEIL *(glancing at her watch)*: Oh, Lord...

> *She runs into the kitchen.*

> *There is a pause. The house is calm. Then, FIXIE bursts in through the front door. He speaks to an unseen JINX.*

FIXIE *(anxiously)*: Sweets, come inside. The neighbors will get the wrong idea. *(Pause)* Come on, hon. Honestly, you'll start all the old biddies gossiping for nothing. Come on in.

> *In walks JINX— in a full, white, veiled, to-beat-the-band wedding gown.*

FIXIE: I still say you're being foolish.

JINX: I am not. I said I was going to be the first to be seen in a wedding dress in your family, and by God, I am! She thinks she can steal the spotlight so easily...

FIXIE *(nervously looking around)*: Keep your voice down. Somebody might still be sleeping.

JINX: Huh! Probably that slug-a-bed sister of yours.

FIXIE: Now, be nice, sweets. Jean's getting married today.

JINX *(triumphantly)*: But I'm wearing the gown!

FIXIE: I don't know why it's so important to you.

JINX: You're a man. You wouldn't.

FIXIE *(lovingly moving toward her)*: But, angel, you know I'm crazy about you. *(He puts his arms around her, suddenly he recoils)* Ow! *(He sucks his finger in pain)* What was that?

JINX: Oh, a straight pin. I had Mama pin me into this dress. You don't think it was ready yet, do you? Mama was up all night just getting the sleeves into the pieces. She had to pin most of it together.

FIXIE *(caressing her arm lovingly)*: Aw, honey, you shouldn't have— *(Suddenly pulls back— another pin attack)* Yikes!

JINX: Just keep your hands off of me and I'll be alright. Okay?

FIXIE: Okay.

> CEIL walks in with a tray of cups and saucers and doughnuts. She places them on a sideboard. She stops, gets a good long look at Jinx.

CEIL: You're... are you—? Who's getting married here today? Do I have to polish more silverware?

FIXIE: No, this is just Jinx's outfit for the wedding.

CEIL: Oh. Well, it's very pretty, honey. Thanks for showing me. But I really think you'd better change into your regular clothes. People are going to start arriving.

JINX: I'm wearing this to the wedding.

CEIL: You mean to your wedding.

JINX: No, to this wedding.

CEIL: Oh. *(She advances to Jinx and lays a gentle hand on her shoulder)* Well, you suit yourself, then— Ow! *(A pin has struck again, Ceil looks at her bleeding hand)* You know, it isn't nice to be so mean.

JINX: My mother pinned me into this dress.

CEIL *(to herself)*: And they say us spinsters are a little wifty...

> MARGUERITE comes down the stairs.

MARGUERITE: What's this?

CEIL: Jinx is going to, er, wear her wedding dress today.

MARGUERITE *(breathless rushing to Jinx)*: A double ceremony!

> She throws her arms around JINX, then screams in pain— she, too, has been stabbed. Multiple times, perhaps.

Aighh! What is that, some kind of booby trap?

JINX: It's not quite finished.

MARGUERITE: Then how can you get married in it?

JINX *(hotly)*: I'm not!

MARGUERITE: I don't get it.

CEIL: Never mind. You look very nice, Marguerite. How's Jean doing?

MARGUERITE: I think she's been nipping at something. She keeps giggling in the bathroom.

CEIL: Nerves. Come on, girls, I still need help in the kitchen.

JINX: I am not doing any kitchen work in my wedding gown.

CEIL: We'll find something... clean for you to do.

As the CEIL, JINX, and MARGUERITE exit to the kitchen:

MARGUERITE: So, let's run this through again— what's with the wedding gown?

FIXIE takes a moment, then places a small wrapped gift box on the sideboard, next to the doughnuts. While he's there, he sneaks a doughnut. JEAN runs down the stairs all dressed in her new outfit.

JEAN: Officer, arrest that doughnut thief!

FIXIE freezes, then proceeds to almost knock over the cups, saucers and doughnuts. JEAN bursts out in giggles— a little too much for the situation.

FIXIE: God! Don't do that!

JEAN: Gotcha!

FIXIE *(good-naturedly)*: If you aren't the worst. *(He gets a good look at her)* You look... really swell, kid. Honest.

JEAN reacts with a whoop of laughter.

What's so funny?

JEAN: I... I don't know. So, where's the groom?

FIXIE *(suddenly panicking)*: I don't know! Was I supposed to pick him up? Is that a best man's job?

JEAN: I don't know. I don't think so.

FIXIE: Do you want me to get him?

JEAN: He's only six doors down, stupid. Give him time. When he finds out who's marrying him, he may turn around and leave anyway.

FIXIE: Relax. Buddy knows you alright.

JEAN: No, I mean when he finds out who's performing the ceremony.

FIXIE: Who?

JEAN: Holy Joe.

FIXIE: No!

JEAN: Yeah.

FIXIE: What happened to Father Brendan?

JEAN: We're not sure, but right now he's sprinkling holy water on some bundles for Britain.

FIXIE: Huh?

JEAN: Holy Joe told him he would marry us. Marguerite was at early Mass this morning, and something's up. I just hope he doesn't start mouthing his mumbo-jumbo about converting. Buddy's a sweet guy, but you can't push him around about God.

FIXIE: I know; once when we were in high school I tried to get him to come with me to church.

JEAN: He's been to our church.

FIXIE: I know. Midnight Mass. But then I made the mistake of asking him if he wanted to be baptized. He said, "I'm already baptized." I said, "No, you're not— not in the eyes of the true Church. " He said, what did it matter, he was still baptized. I told him that he was considered a traitor to God because he didn't revere the Blessed Mother.

JEAN: What did he say?

FIXIE: Nothing. He just pushed me into my locker and wouldn't let me out until I took it back.

JEAN: Did you take it back?

FIXIE: Of course. Twenty minutes later I was in confession taking back what I had just taken back.

He goes for another doughnut, or so JEAN thinks.

JEAN: Hey, lay off the doughnuts.

FIXIE turns around with the gift.

What's this?

FIXIE *(shyly)*: It's for you— and Buddy.

JEAN: Should I wait for Buddy?

FIXIE: Nah, you can open it.

JEAN opens the gift.

JEAN *(quietly)*: I— I don't get it.

FIXIE: It's Mama's prayer book

JEAN: How—?

FIXIE: I stole it from Aunt Mary.

JEAN *(giggling)*: You did? When?

FIXIE: About a year after Mother died. I heard her bragging about how she had it, and that it wasn't worth anything, but her brother had given it to Mother, and it was rightfully hers...

JEAN: How'd you get away with it?

FIXIE: Aw, the old windbag never even noticed it was gone. She had her own precious prayer book. She stuck it in a drawer.

JEAN: Oh, Fixie, no. You should give this to Jinx.

FIXIE: She already has one.

JEAN: Then Marguerite should have it. She's the oldest.

FIXIE: No. I want you to have it. I can't really give you anything else.

JEAN *(shyly hugs him)*: You're...

> *Her shoulders start to shake.*

FIXIE: You're not crying, are you?

> *JEAN pulls her head up. She is giggling.*

Oh, God, here we go.

> *There is a knock at the door. JEAN, recovering herself, goes to answer it.*

JEAN: I just hope Holy Joe keeps his mouth shut except to say, "I now pronounce you man and wife."

> *CAPUTO and NICKI, in their best dresses, hats and gloves, burst through the door.*

NICKI & CAPUTO: We're here!

NICKI: You look like a bandbox!

CAPUTO: Like a million bucks! A million, trillion bucks! *(Hands a large box to Jean)* Here's the corsages and boutonnieres, compliments of Sal.

JEAN: Aw, thanks, kid.

CAPUTO: How do you feel?

> *JEAN answers with an uncontrollable burst of giggles.*

CAPUTO *(dryly)*: Steady as a rock.

> *CEIL enters, scanning the room for anything she may have forgotten.*

CEIL: I'm going up to change. *(She starts upstairs)* Anything that's not done now won't get done.

> *She disappears.*

CAPUTO: Thanks, Ceil. Good to see you, too.

JEAN: Where are the boys?

CAPUTO: Get this—

NICKI: The two of them left Buddy and Fixie after bowling last night and proceeded to tie one on in Buddy's honor. Right, Fixie?

FIXIE: Well...

NICKI: At four this morning each of us got a drunken phone call from Jersey. Seems they were going fishing!

CAPUTO: After a few belts, they must have forgot Buddy's wedding and were on to the good old days, when the two of them were single.

NICKI: And they used to be able to go fishing whenever they wanted.

CAPUTO: So, they informed us two battleaxes that—

NICKI & CAPUTO: —they were going fishing!

CAPUTO: So, here we are. Welcome to married life.

> She gives a start.

Ooh.

NICKI: Not again.

JEAN: What?

CAPUTO: Nothing. It's just that little Angelo has been kicking up a storm all morning.

NICKI: I thought it was Mario.

CAPUTO (another kick): Ooh!

JEAN: You alright, Ange?

CAPUTO: Yeah, yeah. He's just aiming a little lower this morning.

JEAN (nervously): I think I need a cup of coffee... You girls want some?

NICKI & CAPUTO: Sure, yeah.

NICKI: I'll make it.

JEAN (heading for the kitchen door): No, sit. I'll do it. I need something to do.

> She exits. There is a pause. Followed by JEAN's wildest laughter yet— out and out hoots. She has seen JINX.

NICKI & CAPUTO (to Fixie): What—?

> JEAN staggers mirthfully out of the kitchen, helpless with laughter.

CAPUTO: What? What?

> JINX appears in the doorway, livid. MARGUERITE follows, slinks into a chair, catching Jean's giggles. Now it's the other girls' turn to scream with laughter, though they don't quite know why...

JINX (tight-lipped with rage): Fixie! Tell them to quit it!

FIXIE: I... can't, honey. They— you—

> *It's too much. Poor FIXIE doubles over with laughter.*

JINX *(furious)*: Stop it! Stop it!!

> *It only gets funnier. The doorbell rings. Jean goes to the door, opens it, all of them still laughing away. In the doorway looms a forbidding, middle-aged monsignor. Uh-oh. It's HOLY JOE.*

JEAN *(after recognizing the apparition's identity, shouts to all)*: Jesus Christ, it's Holy Joe!

> *This shuts everyone up— in horror. And rather belatedly, all the Catholics do the quick head-bow.*

JEAN: I mean, Holy Christ, I... I mean... good morning, Monsignor McDonough.

HOLY JOE: Good morning, Regina.

> *The OTHER FIVE mumble, "Good morning, Father."*

HOLY JOE *(acknowledging each in his or her turn)*: Angela, Ludmila, Genevieve, Francis Xavier, Margaret.

MARGUERITE *(quietly)*: Reet.

HOLY JOE: I beg your pardon?

MARGUERITE: It's Margue-REET, Father.

HOLY JOE: Yes? *(Awkward pause)* Where is the intended bridegroom? He seems to be missing all the fun.

JEAN: He's still getting dressed, Father.

HOLY JOE: How do you know that?

JEAN: Oh, I don't. I just assumed. He's still down the street. At his house. Please, come in. Marguerite, would you see if there's coffee for Father?

MARGUERITE: Maybe he doesn't want coffee. Would you like coffee, Father?

HOLY JOE: Please.

> *MARGUERITE beats a hasty retreat to the kitchen.*

JEAN: Please, sit down, Father.

HOLY JOE *(looking around)*: Has this house been blessed?

JEAN: Gee, I don't know. It's been in my cousin's Ceil's family for twenty-five years.

HOLY JOE: Were her unfortunate parents good Catholics?

JEAN: Oh, yes, Father.

> *He seems to subtly relax and takes a seat.*

HOLY JOE *(noticing Jinx's outfit)*: Genevieve, I wasn't aware that you were getting married today.

JINX: I'm not, Father.

HOLY JOE: I don't understand.

JINX: Understand what, Father?

CAPUTO: Why you're in that get-up.

JINX: I... I... was trying it out.

> *She takes a few paces, as if checking out the gown's "walkability." Just as she moves her arms a bit to check out the sleeves, they both pop their pins, falling off her arms. She clutches them, mortified.*

Excuse me Father.

> *She runs into the kitchen.*

HOLY JOE: You're all excused. I'd like to speak with Regina alone.

> *They all head quickly for the kitchen door, answering, "Sure, Father," "Of course," "You bet." FIXIE, in the lead, pushes the kitchen door. We hear a crash of china, followed by—*

MARGUERITE *(from kitchen)*: Oh, God damn it! Will you watch where you're going?

> *They all rush, sheepishly, through the door.*

HOLY JOE: I can see that a visit to your home yields a much more colorful picture than the one your family presents at church.

JEAN: Well, you know how it is, Father. Church brings out the best in people. *(She emits a gust of raucous giggles)* Sorry, Father.

HOLY JOE: Regina—

JEAN: Yes, Father?

HOLY JOE: Simmer down.

JEAN: Yes, Father.

HOLY JOE: Before your intended gets here, I'd like to be clarified on a few points. Until my mind is clear, I can't perform the ceremony.

> *JEAN bursts out in giggles again.*

Regina, pull yourself together.

JEAN: Yes, Father. I'm sorry. I'm a little nervous with all this. *(Composes herself)* What do you need to know?

HOLY JOE: Have you made a confession lately?

JEAN: Oh, yes, Father. Yesterday. I wanted to come into my marriage free of sin.

HOLY JOE: Well, you've had all morning to stain your soul. Don't think it's that easy to keep sin away.

JEAN: Well, let's say I'm trying my best.

HOLY JOE: Has your intended finished his instruction from Father Brendan?

JEAN: Oh, yes, Father.

HOLY JOE: And does he know more than the batting average of the Phillies starting lineup?

> *JEAN screams with laughter. A look from HOLY JOE quiets her down.*

JEAN: He knows everything he needs to know, I think.

HOLY JOE: Perhaps a quick quiz when he arrives will be in order.

JEAN: Oh, no, Father. I don't think that'll be necessary. He understands. And he respects my right to believe in... what we believe in.

HOLY JOE: Is there any possibility that he'll convert?

JEAN: I don't— *(Thinks better of her response)* Well, there's always the possibility... And I suppose the quicker we're married the faster he might... be filled with the Holy Ghost.

HOLY JOE: We can hope and pray. And he'll consent to raising your children Catholic?

JEAN: Yes, Father.

HOLY JOE: Well, with all you young people racing to get married these days before... Mr. Tojo and Mr. Hitler impose their Godless ways, it seems as much as we can ask for.

> *JEAN visibly relaxes. HOLY JOE produces a document from his pocket.*

And we'll make it official with this contract.

JEAN: What's that?

> *BUDDY enters, all dressed up, and immediately runs to his usual spot and does his usual headstand.*

BUDDY *(singing)*:
NOT A SOUL DOWN ON THE CORNER,
THAT'S A PRETTY CERTAIN SIGN
THOSE WEDDING BELLS ARE BREAKING UP
THAT OLD GANG OF MINE.
> *(He leaps up and kisses Jean)*

Hiya, gorgeous. *(Sees Holy Joe)* Holy—

JEAN: Buddy, you remember Monsignor McDonough.

BUDDY: Yes, sure. Hello, Father.

JEAN: Father Brendan was called away. Monsignor McDonough will be marrying us.

BUDDY: Ah, jeez. What happened to Father Brendan? Is he okay?

HOLY JOE: He's fine.

JEAN: He has to bless some ships.

> *Looks meaningfully at BUDDY.*

BUDDY: Huh?

HOLY JOE: He's doing Our Lord's work down at the shipyard.

BUDDY: Can't he get back in time?

HOLY JOE: I'm afraid not. Sit down, please.

BUDDY sits.

BUDDY: We can wait a little bit. We're due down Ocean City, but they'll hold the reservation until tonight.

HOLY JOE: I'm here because I have some questions to put to you.

BUDDY: Fire away, Father.

HOLY JOE: I will also be quite frank with you. I have grave doubts as to the appropriateness of this marriage. Did Father Brendan counsel you on the joys you would experience if you were a Catholic?

BUDDY *(after looking at Jean, quizzically)*: Oh, yeah!

HOLY JOE: And yet you remain... unmoved.

BUDDY: Well, you see, Father, I grew up the grandson of a Baptist minister.

HOLY JOE: Oh, dear. I had no idea it was this serious. You're a Baptist?

BUDDY: No!

HOLY JOE: I don't follow.

BUDDY: My father left his father's house under, a dark cloud, you might say. And, so, my dad sort of fell away from religion altogether by the time we kids were born.

HOLY JOE: So, you are... unbaptized?

BUDDY: No! When I was sixteen, I went to church with some of my friends— hey, I even went to Mass once with Fixie!

HOLY JOE: Fixie?

JEAN: My brother, father— Francis Xavier. He's Buddy's best friend. They call him Fixie.

HOLY JOE: Oh. What a vulgar sobriquet.

BUDDY: Well, one pal of mine went to a Presbyterian church. He took me along one week. I listened to a great guy, Reverend Foster, talk all about... well, I don't know— optimism, how God gives us all brains to think with, hearts to feel with, and bodies to take care of the two. Simple things. He got to me, that's the only way I can explain it. I sometimes think I was lucky, skipping all the Bible stories and baptisms when I was too young to think for myself. Now, when I read anything, I can use that brain God gave us and think it through. And when I finally got baptized by Reverend Foster, it meant something. Well, I guess Reverend Foster's a lot like you, Father. He's there whenever my opinion bumps up against something the church says. I go and ask him, and he listens to me. Most of the time, he says, "Well, Buddy, you're thinking and you're feeling. Don't let the fine print stop you."

HOLY JOE: How... homespun.

BUDDY: Now, your religion is beautiful. I love the smells of the incense, the loud music, the gorgeous windows. And, when Jean and I talk about religion, we seem to agree ninety-nine percent of the time. We just... don't let the fine print stop us, I guess...

HOLY JOE: Well, speaking of fine print—

> *A procession of meek penitents emerges from the kitchen: MARGUERITE, gingerly holding a tray with coffee and cups, is followed by CAPUTO, NICKI, CEIL, FIXIE and JINX.*

JINX *(picks up a cup and saucer, hands it to Holy Joe)*: Coffee, Father?

> *At this point, JINX's bodice decides to bust out of their pinned-in moorings, leaving her midsection exposed. She shrieks and runs into the kitchen, bumping into MARGUERITE and causing Marguerite to drop the coffee tray. CEIL is aghast.*

MARGUERITE: Ah, shit!!!!!

> *She exits.*

JEAN *(after a painful silence)*: How do you take your coffee, Father?

HOLY JOE *(witheringly)*: Black.

JEAN: What were you about to say, Father?

BUDDY: Something about fine print—

CAPUTO: I'm sorry. If you're not finished, we can—

NICKI: —go back to the kitchen.

FIXIE: Yeah, and I'll see if Jinx— Genevieve— is okay— no, I can't see her like that— maybe—

CEIL: I'll check and see.

HOLY JOE: Everyone, just be quiet! Find a seat and light there!

> *Everyone obeys quickly.*

Now then—

> *The kitchen door opens a crack. JINX, clutching the fabric cutouts to her bodice close to her, appears, hissing—*

JINX: Pssst! Nicki! Ceil!

> *All eyes turn to her, including HOLY JOE.*

HOLY JOE: Genevieve! Get in here!

> *We hear unintelligible sobs of protest from JINX.*

Now!

> *JINX slinks in, moving to position of concealment behind an armchair.*

HOLY JOE (CONT'D): I am trying to solicit this young man's signature on this document.

BUDDY: Oh, we already have the marriage license, Father.

JEAN (nervously— she senses something's up): And the blood test— everything. We even have a lease on a new apartment. We're lousy with documents.

HOLY JOE: This is different. Read it, Regina.

She takes it and reads.

JEAN: "I do hereby attest to the Archdiocese of Philadelphia, through its witness, Monsignor Aloysius McDonough, that I will affirm, uphold and do all in my power to defend the faith of my beloved wife."

There is a sigh of relief.

(To Holy Joe)

So, you're not asking Buddy to convert?

HOLY JOE: Will you?

BUDDY: Sorry, Father.

CEIL: You're just asking him to sign this paper saying that it's alright for Jean to practice her religion.

HOLY JOE: Finish reading, Regina.

JEAN: "I also attest that any progeny of this union shall be baptized and raised as Roman Catholic."

CAPUTO: You've already agreed to that, haven't you, Buddy?

BUDDY: Yep.

JEAN: So, this is just a form from the church whenever someone marries a non-Catholic, right?

HOLY JOE: No.

JEAN: No?

HOLY JOE (proudly): I drew it up myself.

JEAN: Well, who's it for?

HOLY JOE: Everyone. It simply puts on the record what has been promised to Our Lord.

JEAN: Who would hold on to it, Father?

HOLY JOE: I would. I'll keep it under official church records, just as I would with any marriage between two Catholics.

JEAN: Well, I guess there's no harm in it.

HOLY JOE: No harm? I should hope not. This is imperative. I will not perform the ceremony without his signature on this document.

All eyes on BUDDY.

BUDDY (slowly): Well, Father, we got a problem. Because I won't sign it.

General surprise.

JEAN: What?

BUDDY: Honey, I love you. I love you and I respect you. I respect your right to worship. That's the American way. And I know how important it is to you. And I also know that kids have a way of growing up and finding their own way, no matter what religion they're taught. Now, I've given my word that you and any kids we have will be raised Catholic. My word has to be good enough.

JEAN *(on the verge of tears)*: Honey, it is good enough for me, but couldn't you just—

BUDDY: Nope.

JEAN *(tensely)*: Father won't marry us unless—

BUDDY: There are only two people I'm afraid of in this world. One of them is my father.

CEIL: Amen.

BUDDY: And the other's Adolf Hitler. One I have to obey and the other I hope never to meet. You, Father, don't exert that kind of influence over me, I'm sorry to say.

HOLY JOE: Well, then, I'm sorry to say that's all we have to discuss.

> *He rises and heads for the door, followed by JEAN, CAPUTO, NICKI and CEIL.*

CAPUTO: Please, Father. These two really love each other.

HOLY JOE: I'm sorry.

NICKI: Father, his word really is important.

MARGUERITE *(to Buddy)*: So, when the chips are down, this is how you treat us.

BUDDY: Treat who?

JEAN *(to Marguerite)*: Be quiet.

HOLY JOE: If you change your mind, you know where the rectory is.

> *He opens the door to leave— standing in the doorway is a very anxious middle-aged LADY in a housedress.*

MRS. SINCLAIR: I haven't missed it, have I?

BUDDY: Mom!

MRS. SINCLAIR: Oh, please say I haven't. Are you Father Brendan? I thought you were a much younger man.

HOLY JOE: I am Monsignor McDonough.

MRS. SINCLAIR: Oh! How do you do! Oh, good, Father Brendan isn't here yet. *(To Holy Joe, anxiously)* Quick, come inside!

> *She hustles HOLY JOE inside and closes the door.*

BUDDY: Mom, what are you doing here?

MRS. SINCLAIR: I ran out the back way. Your father's asleep. He won't be up until after you're married— if God is the kind and benevolent being I believe him to be. What do you think, Father?

HOLY JOE: I'm afraid your husband will have to be in a coma to sleep until these two have been married.

BUDDY': He means there's a hitch, Mom.

MRS. SINCLAIR: A hitch? What kind of hitch?

JEAN *(through a sudden wave of giggles)*: He... doesn't... want to... marry us! Buddy... *(A string of giggles)* refuses to sign a paper.

MRS. SINCLAIR: What kind of paper?

HOLY JOE: Affirming Regina's rights to practice her religion.

MRS. SINCLAIR: Oh, heavens, he doesn't have to sign a paper about that!

BUDDY: Thanks, Mom.

MRS. SINCLAIR: I'll sign it.

HOLY JOE: What?

MRS. SINCLAIR: I'm his mother. I signed for him when he needed a loan to start his business. Of course, I signed my husband's name— he wouldn't co-sign anything. He's a very... cautious man. Of course, please don't think that makes me a dishonest woman— or that my signature isn't valid. It is. I'm very honest. Give me the paper, Father.

HOLY JOE: I can't do that.

MRS. SINCLAIR *(gravely)*: Please, Father, my husband is only sure to sleep 'til eleven.

HOLY JOE: I can't let you do that.

MRS. SINCLAIR *(sternly)*: Buddy?

BUDDY: Yes, Mom?

MRS. SINCLAIR: Sign the paper.

BUDDY: I'm sorry. I can't.

MRS. SINCLAIR *(urgently)*: Walter, sign that paper.

> *JEAN begins to giggle furiously as the tension builds. By the end of this scene she should barely be able to contain herself.*

BUDDY: No, ma'am, I can't.

MRS. SINCLAIR: Father, let me sign that paper.

HOLY JOE: I'm sorry. I'll have to leave now.

> *He again heads for the door.*

CEIL: Father— I know you don't know me well. I'm Jean's cousin. I own this house. I— haven't been to Mass regularly, but I believe most heartily in the Father, the Son and the Holy Ghost. And in front of them, and everyone here, I have to tell you that this is not fair.

HOLY JOE: You're right, Miss. I don't know you. Please excuse me.

CAPUTO (lurching forward): Father—

HOLY JOE: Not now, Angela.

CAPUTO: Father, listen to me!

HOLY JOE: I will not be spoken to like this!

CAPUTO (suddenly yelps with pain): What does labor feel like?

> The assembled now spring into action, with most of the following dialogue overlapping:

CEIL: Oh, my God! Call the doctor!

CAPUTO: Seven months, my ass!

NICKI: Take it easy, kid.

BUDDY: I'll take you to the hospital. Fixie, go get a taxi!

> FIXIE runs out the front door.

CEIL: Marguerite, boil some water, just in case.

> MARGUERITE tears into the kitchen.

JINX: What should I do?

CEIL: Hold yourself together.

NICKI: You alright, Ange?

CAPUTO: I don't know. Get me outta here!

> FIXIE runs back in, ashen. He's scared— and virtually speechless.

FIXIE: Uh... uh— your— your...

BUDDY: What?

FIXIE: Your father's on his way!

> Everyone freezes for a second.

CAPUTO: Holy shit!

> Blackout.

END OF ACT I

ACT II

*The scene is exactly as we left it. JINX is clasping her hands
to her midsection. NICKI and CEIL are attending to CAPUTO.
JEAN is helplessly hysterical. FIXIE is backed up against the
door, gasping in fright. MRS. SINCLAIR, HOLY JOE and BUDDY
are in equal states of terror and confusion.*

FIXIE: I mean it! He's coming down the street! His right cheek is all bunched up!

BUDDY and MRS. SINCLAIR.

Oh, no.

HOLY JOE *(in spite of himself he catches the general wave of panic)*: What does that mean?

MRS. SINCLAIR: My husband is not a happy man to begin with, Father. But when he's especially in a snit, he bunches up his cheek like this. *(She demonstrates)* And now, if you'll all excuse me, I'll run out the back way. I was never here— remember that!

She shoves open the kitchen door. An almighty crash. And—

MARGUERITE'S VOICE: GOD DAMN IT TO HELL!

CEIL *(calling to Marguerite)*: Are you alright, Marguerite?

MARGUERITE'S VOICE: I was just bringing in some GODDAMN BOWLS for the GODDAMN WATER I'M BOILING!!

HOLY JOE: Margaret! Your language!

MARGUERITE *(storms out the kitchen door, livid)*: Reet! Reet! My goddamn name is Margue-RITE!

She goes back into the kitchen.

*There is an insistent knock on the front door. Everyone
freezes. Cold. There is a pause. Then another knock. Nothing.
No reaction from anyone. Just blind fear.*

CAPUTO *(quietly)*: This is amazing.

EVERYONE: Sshhh!

CAPUTO: Even the kid's afraid of him. I think I'm okay.

A very insistent knock.

MR. SINCLAIR'S VOICE: Miss O'Connell!

Everyone looks at CEIL, who looks stricken.

Miss O'Connell! This is Ezra Sinclair! Is marriage going on in there?

CEIL *(finding her voice after much difficulty)*: N-no, Mr. Sinclair. Not as of yet.

MR. SINCLAIR'S VOICE: Will you let me in, please?

> *CEIL walks with dread to the door. Suddenly, she makes a steely decision— to lie.*

CEIL: Your son isn't here, Mr. Sinclair, if that's who you're looking for.

> *The room stares in amazement at CEIL's boldness.*

MR. SINCLAIR'S VOICE: And my wife?

CEIL: Why would she be here?

MR. SINCLAIR'S VOICE: Our son is fixing to have a wedding in there today, ain't he?

CEIL: Y-yes.

MR. SINCLAIR'S VOICE: Well, she's not at home. And it's my breakfast time. Either she ran off with the milkman, or she's here. Believe me, Miss O'Connell, the milkman knows me better than you do.

CEIL: I thought you slept 'til eleven.

MR. SINCLAIR'S VOICE: Well, generally, I do, but— what the hell do you know about my sleeping habits?

CEIL: Nothing, I—

MR. SINCLAIR'S VOICE: Let me the hell in so I can speak to my son when he gets there. He's probably out somewhere with that Papist son-of-a-bitch he calls his best friend.

> *FIXIE is shocked. So— so very much so— is HOLY JOE.*

HOLY JOE: How dare you, sir!

MR. SINCLAIR'S VOICE: Who the hell is that?

HOLY JOE: My name is Monsignor Aloysius McDonough.

MR. SINCLAIR'S VOICE: Another Papist son-of-a-bitch...

HOLY JOE *(opening the door in a rage)*: You get in here and say that to my face!

> *MR. SINCLAIR enters. He's wearing a suit, but with just an old-fashioned Union suit undershirt under the jacket. He could use a shave. His countenance— especially with that bunching cheek action— is the epitome of the word "sourpuss." Everyone has frozen with fear once again.*

MR. SINCLAIR *(spotting Mrs. Sinclair)*: What the hell is this?

MRS. SINCLAIR: Hello, Ezra.

MR. SINCLAIR *(feigning nonchalance)*: Do you know something, Sophie?

MRS. SINCLAIR: What's that?

MR. SINCLAIR: You're not home.

MRS. SINCLAIR: Well, I—

MR. SINCLAIR: You're not home, Sophie!

MRS. SINCLAIR: I know, Ezra. I was hoping... well, that—

MR. SINCLAIR: You were hoping what, that I'd died in my sleep? What gives here? *(To Ceil)* You. You told me my son and my wife weren't here!

CEIL: I realize that, Mr. Sinclair. I'm sorry. And, Father, I plan to do penance just as soon as I can get to church.

HOLY JOE: I have a feeling before this day is out, there'll be a positive parade to the confessional.

MR. SINCLAIR: Who the hell are all you people?

CAPUTO *(dryly)*: The Unwed Mothers of West Philly.

JINX: We are not! *(Marches right up to Mr. Sinclair)* And I do not appreciate your calling my husband-to-be such a dirty name. We're all good Catholics here!

> *Unfortunately, her statement is punctuated at this precise moment by the sudden bursting of the rest of her dress. Her dress falls off her in an instant, leaving her is a short slip, bra and girdle. She screams, runs up the stairs and exits, mortified.*

CAPUTO: Uh, by the way, if anyone's interested, I think the crisis is over. *(Smiling, to Nicki)* I'm enjoying this more than you know. *(To her belly)* Stay right where you are, kid.

MR. SINCLAIR *(to Buddy and Mrs. Sinclair)*: Let's go.

BUDDY: No, Dad.

MR. SINCLAIR: Don't you dare contradict me!

BUDDY *(quivering but steadfast)*: I'm sorry, Dad. *(Moves to Jean, putting his arm around her)* But this is the girl I'm going to marry.

> *JEAN can't hold it in— she lets out an unforgettable howl of cackles.*

MR. SINCLAIR: She's nuts.

BUDDY: She's nervous.

MR. SINCLAIR: She's a lunatic.

BUDDY: She's afraid.

MR. SINCLAIR: She's a Catholic. Stop arguing with me. Come on.

BUDDY: I can't. Mom, you tell him.

MRS. SINCLAIR: Ezra—

MR. SINCLAIR: Oh, God.

MRS. SINCLAIR: Ezra, dear...

MR. SINCLAIR: Sophie.

MRS. SINCLAIR: Yes, Ezra?

MR. SINCLAIR: Tell these good people what my father did for a living.

MRS. SINCLAIR: He was a Baptist minister.

MR. SINCLAIR: And tell them what he is now.

MRS. SINCLAIR: Not... alive.

MR. SINCLAIR: He's dead, Sophie. The son-of-a-bitch is dead.

MRS. SINCLAIR: Yes, dear.

MR. SINCLAIR: Tell the good people what he said when I left the farm and came to Philly.

MRS. SINCLAIR: He said you'd suffer the eternal flames of hell.

MR. SINCLAIR: What did I say?

MRS. SINCLAIR: Nothing.

MR. SINCLAIR: That is right. Until the day he died. I never spoke to him again. *(To Holy Joe)* You.

HOLY JOE: Are you addressing me?

MR. SINCLAIR: Yes, you! I think Catholics are a bunch of mumbo-jumbo Mary worshipers. Will I suffer the eternal flames of hell?

HOLY JOE: You most certainly will.

MR. SINCLAIR: This is your lucky day, fella. You get something I never gave my daddy. A final word. Kiss my ass.

HOLY JOE: That's it. I cannot stay and put up with abuse. Let me out of here. Regina, I expect to hear from you later today— as a single, Catholic woman! *(He stalks to the door, to Mr. Sinclair)* And, as for you, sir, your son will never know peace with a father like you!

MR. SINCLAIR: What the hell are fathers for?

> *HOLY JOE exits in a huff. MR. SINCLAIR goes out to make sure he's really gone. JEAN walks slowly, silently, to a chair.*

JEAN: Well, the giggles are gone.

CAPUTO: Why? This is the worst part yet. *(Winces with pain)* Ooh. Damn it.

JEAN: What's to be nervous about now? It's over. I'm not getting married.

BUDDY *(going to her)*: Aw, don't say that.

JEAN: You don't want to marry me, do you?

BUDDY: I do! Honest to God, I do. I just have to have something about this marriage deal that's mine. I can't sign my name to some made-up contract. I can't.

JEAN: I don't want you to. *(Looks him straight in the eye)* So, we're stuck.

MRS. SINCLAIR: Don't be blue, honey. Love will find a way.

> *MR. SINCLAIR comes in from the porch.*

MR. SINCLAIR: Sophie! I said let's go. The girl's a lunatic.

MRS. SINCLAIR: She's not, Ezra. And you know it. You remember her mother. She was the same way. And she was the sweetest person.

JEAN *(to Mrs. Sinclair)*: I never heard you talk about my mother before. I never heard you talk this much before.

MRS. SINCLAIR *(searching for an explanation)*: Well, it's a special occasion.

MR. SINCLAIR: Sophie...

JEAN: You remember my mother?

MRS. SINCLAIR: Oh my, yes. We used to say hello when she'd pass by with all three of you. *(Laughs)* She looked like a mother hen. Marguerite was wobbling beside her, Francis was in the buggy, and you were in her arms. She'd always say "good morning." I loved the slow way she'd say it, to hide that little trace of an accent. She tried so hard to be American, but there was a little... something that made her sound, well... foreign, I guess you'd say. And she had your hair. Or, I guess you have hers.

JEAN *(sadly)*: I have her troubles now, too.

MRS. SINCLAIR: Oh, honey. Everybody has troubles these days.

MR. SINCLAIR *(to Mrs. Sinclair)*: And yours is looking you in the face. Let's go home.

MRS. SINCLAIR: Buddy? You coming?

MR. SINCLAIR: Of course he is.

BUDDY: Dad?

MR. SINCLAIR: What?

BUDDY: Kiss my ass.

> *After a moment, it hits him. His son has just said, "kiss my ass." He erupts in a rage, furiously pulling his belt off, brandishing it like a whip, and chasing BUDDY around the living room.*

MR. SINCLAIR: What the hell did you say? Why... why... what the HELL did you say to me? Come here— get over here— stand still, you little shitass. I'll show you who's gonna kiss your ass. Get—

BUDDY *(really scared)*: I... thought you'd appreciate that remark! I'm standing up to you! Don't you respect that? I guess not. Dad, Dad! Stop! Listen to me, please!

> *MR. SINCLAIR freezes, snorting like a mad bull.*

MR. SINCLAIR: This better be good.

BUDDY: I'm sorry, Dad. Please, just go home, and, and... cool down. I'll be home in five minutes. I promise.

> *After a moment of consideration, MR. SINCLAIR lunges for BUDDY.*

MR. SINCLAIR: Not good enough!

The chase is on again. Finally, MRS. SINCLAIR comes between her son and her husband.

MRS. SINCLAIR: Ezra! Let's go home, please! I'll make waffles!

MR. SINCLAIR *(very winded)*: You're damn right, you'll make waffles. And make enough for him. *(To Buddy)* They'll be ready in five minutes! Let's go, Sophie. Goodbye, all. *(Stops at door, to Buddy)* Five minutes!

MRS. SINCLAIR: It was very nice seeing you all.

They leave. Everyone is visibly relieved.

NICKI: I don't get it.

CEIL: What?

NICKI: If your father doesn't believe in anything, what does he care if you marry a Catholic?

BUDDY: You tell me.

JEAN: It's just an excuse. He doesn't like me, that's all.

CEIL: He doesn't even know you, honey. I remember when your mother was alive, too. He liked her enough then. At least, they always said hello, just like Mrs. Sinclair said.

CAPUTO: Gee, they were practically family.

BUDDY: My father just doesn't like anybody who's different.

FIXIE: Who does?

BUDDY: I do. I think "different" usually means "interesting." Something new. Don't you?

Everyone looks at him quizzically.

CEIL: There's different and then there's different.

BUDDY: What do you mean?

CEIL: I don't know— maybe it's Jean's mother's side. You know, we've got a little Dutchman in us. And that old doughboy might just think we're made up of enemy parts.

BUDDY *(to Jean)*: What did you mean when you said now you had your mother's troubles?

JEAN: Just what Ceil said. Old blood thinking. My mother was an immigrant.

BUDDY: So was your father.

JEAN & CEIL: Oh, no he wasn't!

JEAN: Are you kidding? Ask Aunt Mary if you don't believe me. See, they came over as babies. From a country that spoke English. My mother was sixteen when she came over. And she didn't speak English like the shanty Irish.

CEIL: And she had pierced ears! She always wore button earrings to hide it.

JEAN: Yeah, and one day Aunt Mary saw Mother take one of them off because they were pinching her. The old girl yelled out, "Jesus,

Head-bow by all except BUDDY.

JEAN (CONT'D): Mary and Joseph, she's a Gypsy!" Even when Mother died, Aunt Mary didn't want her buried next to her precious brother. Thank God for Aunt Rae.

BUDDY: I like Aunt Rae. Is she coming?

JEAN: Well, no... I was just afraid the more people who knew, the more chance Aunt Mary would come. Of course, I guess it doesn't matter now.

She tears up. CAPUTO, CEIL and NICKI crowd around her.

CEIL: Come on now, sweetie.

CAPUTO: We'll think of some way out of this, kid. *(Bends over and talks to her belly)* You got any ideas? And stop that kickin'!

NICKI: Maybe we can find a... a freelance priest.

The THREE look at her. They suddenly burst out laughing.

JEAN: Wouldn't help, but thanks.

NICKI: How do you know?

JEAN: You don't think the thought occurred to me?

The FOUR laugh again.

Turns out you need some sort of special okay. Even being married in this house was part of the deal with Holy Joe... Or so I thought...

MARGUERITE'S VOICE: Is it okay to come out?

JEAN: Yes.

MARGUERITE comes out warily.

MARGUERITE: Is he gone?

JEAN: He's gone.

MARGUERITE: Oh, shit, am I in trouble. What did I miss?

JEAN: Nothing. The wedding of the century will not take place today.

MARGUERITE: Maybe now I can be the first one to get married.

CAPUTO: Nice, Marguerite. Very nice.

JINX'S VOICE: I am getting married first.

She appears, in a robe, on the stairs. The veil, however, is still on her head.

CAPUTO: Oh, knock it off, for God's sake. *(To Jean)* Yo, kid. You alright?

JEAN: Can... can I talk to Buddy alone?

CAPUTO: Sure. Come on, troops. I think I'd like to lie down. Upstairs.

JEAN: Caputo?

CAPUTO: Yeah?

JEAN: How's the baby?

CAPUTO *(checking her abdomen)*: Hanging on to hear how it all comes out. *(She winks, herding everyone upstairs)* Come on, kids. Let's all grab a needle and sew this one back into her dress. First, we're gonna sew her lips shut.

> They all exit upstairs. BUDDY and JEAN look at each other sadly, shyly.

BUDDY: I wish I knew what to do.

JEAN: Me, too.

BUDDY: I guess this is what being an adult is all about. Not marriage or jobs or houses, but this.

JEAN: What do you mean?

BUDDY: Oh, working it all out. Finding out if you can live with all the rules. Figuring out if the rules are good, or if you should break them and face the consequences. *(Gets an idea)* Take off your shoes.

JEAN: Huh?

BUDDY: Take off your shoes. *(She does)* Now, step on top of my feet.

JEAN: I don't get it.

BUDDY: Like we're going to dance. Didn't you ever do this when you were a little girl?

JEAN: With who, Sister Mary Clara?

BUDDY: Okay, now, let's dance.

> They fox trot a little with Jean's feet solidly on Buddy's.

How does that feel?

JEAN: I don't know. Because you're making all the moves. I don't have to worry about stepping on your toes. I'm already on them.

BUDDY: Now, keep dancing.

> He hoists her up on the sofa, slips off his shoes, steps up himself, so that they're both dancing on the sofa awkwardly.

JEAN: Ceil will have a fit if she sees this.

BUDDY: How do you feel now?

JEAN: Shaky.

BUDDY: Why?

JEAN: Because I've got my feet on the couch!

BUDDY: And it's not right.

JEAN: Yeah.

BUDDY: It's against the rules.

JEAN: Right.

BUDDY: But it's fun, isn't it?

JEAN: I guess.

BUDDY: So you still feel like a bad little kid, right?

JEAN: Right.

BUDDY: What else?

JEAN: What do you mean, what else?

BUDDY: What's it like, dancing up here?

JEAN *(thinking)*: Hard. Tricky. Clumsy.

BUDDY: Feel like you're gonna fall?

JEAN: Sorta.

BUDDY: Me, too. Ever danced up here before?

JEAN: No!

BUDDY: Me neither. Know anybody who has?

JEAN: No.

BUDDY: Me neither. *(He stops dancing, holds her in his arms)* That's what it feels like. All the time lately. Like I'm doing things nobody's ever done before. Like there's nobody who can tell me how to do this. Father Brendan's supposed to tell me things about marrying a Catholic girl, and he winds up talking about baseball. Holy Joe comes up with some paper he dreamed up himself, that even your church hasn't thought up. My father acts as if I'm absolutely crazy. It's like...

JEAN: Like dancing on somebody's good couch?

BUDDY: Exactly! And yet I know there's nothing wrong with this. I mean, nothing really deep-down crazy. Maybe everybody doesn't dance up here, but— is it really all that horrible?

JEAN: We could wreck the springs.

BUDDY: So could your Aunt Mary if she sat on it too quick, but that would be okay.

JEAN: So... our feet are wrong, but Aunt Mary's ass is okay, huh?

> They laugh tenderly, which turns into a big, long kiss. Then
> JEAN sits on the sofa, looking sad.

We're still not married.

BUDDY *(sitting down next to her)*: Reverend Foster would marry us.

JEAN *(sighs)*: Why can't I let him? Will you tell me that? I was the biggest hellion at St. Vincent's. I broke the rules all the time! I do not get along with priests and nuns. I played so many tricks on them I'm surprised word hasn't spread to the Vatican.

BUDDY: Father Brendan and you get along.

JEAN: He's just a nice fella— who happens to be a priest.

BUDDY: Honey. Reverend Foster's just a nice fella who happens to be a minister.

JEAN: I know! Why do I have to be married by a priest? Is it all those years of dreaming about a wedding? I know it's silly, but those daydreams carried me through a lot of cold nights in the dormitory. Specially right after Mother died. They kept me from going crazy during sewing class when I wanted to be out playing basketball.

BUDDY: But you also dreamed about being Amelia Earhart.

JEAN: True.

BUDDY: You even bought that dumb jacket.

JEAN: It is not dumb. It's very smart. It's an imitation leather aviatrix outfit in honor of Amelia. Don't you make fun of that jacket.

BUDDY: Well, which will it be?

JEAN: What do you mean?

BUDDY: Are you going to march down the cathedral in a white dress, or are you going to fly into the wild blue yonder?

JEAN: Amelia never came back.

BUDDY: No, she never did, honey.

JEAN: It's not just the white dress. I do believe in God, you know.

BUDDY: Me, too.

JEAN: And I want us to be really, really married.

BUDDY: Me too. What do you think God thinks?

JEAN: I don't know.

BUDDY (gets a sudden thought): Who made you?

JEAN: What?

BUDDY: Who made you?

JEAN (by rote): God made me.

BUDDY: Why did God make you?

JEAN: To know him, to love him and to serve him— what is this?

BUDDY: Who is God?

JEAN: God is the Supreme Being.

BUDDY: Who made you?

JEAN: God made me.

BUDDY: Who loves you?

JEAN: G-God loves... Wait, that's not in the catechism.

BUDDY: Who loves you?

JEAN: I-I don't know.

BUDDY: Don't you?

JEAN: God?

BUDDY: Does he?

JEAN: Yes. Yes!

BUDDY: Who else?

JEAN: You.

BUDDY: Who made me?

JEAN: God made you.

BUDDY: Who loves me?

JEAN: I love you.

BUDDY: Who else?

JEAN: God.

BUDDY: So, who's stopping us from getting married?

JEAN *(after considering it all, joyfully)*: Well, it sure as hell isn't God, for God's sake!

BUDDY: It's the old man.

JEAN: Both the old men.

BUDDY: And Aunt Mary.

JEAN: By proxy through Marguerite.

BUDDY *(looking around)*: Well, none of them are here. *(He kisses Jean, comfortingly)* I love you, honey. I really do. I don't think God is our enemy. I want you to see Him the way you do— and I want to see Him my way. But— the point is— I think He sees it our way. What do you think?

JEAN: I think you're right. I love you. *(She kisses him)* Now, who the hell do we get to marry us?

> A knock at the door. JEAN answers it. It's MRS. SINCLAIR,
> who pops her head in through the door.

MRS. SINCLAIR: Buddy? Please, honey, I told your father to take a nap. The waffles will wait. From all the excitement, he went out like a light. Hurry home before he finds out I've escaped again!

BUDDY: No, Mom. I found out something just now. Dad isn't God.

MRS. SINCLAIR: He's not?

BUDDY: Nope. Know how I know?

MRS. SINCLAIR: How?

BUDDY *(winking at Jean)*: God made me.

MRS. SINCLAIR: So did your father.

BUDDY: God loves me.

MRS. SINCLAIR: Oh, your Dad does too, sweetie. Deep down.

BUDDY *(triumphantly)*: But God wants me to marry Jean!

MRS. SINCLAIR *(letting this sink in)*: Oh. Well, that must be it, then. You're so clever, hon.

BUDDY: Mom, do you want me to marry Jean?

MRS. SINCLAIR: I want you to be happy.

BUDDY: Same thing.

MRS. SINCLAIR: Then, I want you to marry Jean. *(The floodgates open, she comes into the living room)* Oh, Jean, honey, I'm so sorry. I've always liked you. You're funny and you're sweet. And you'll keep him in line. Not that he needs that much keeping in line. But you'll stand up to him. Not like... me. You'll listen, too. Really listen. Like, like an A student listens to a teacher. Hard. With questions. And I think you'll teach him a thing or two, too. Oh, sweetie, I wish I could tell your Mama and Dad how much I liked them. And how wonderfully you turned out. Forgive a foolish old housewife her husband. He isn't God. But he runs everything. I'm... just sorry. And... well, I'm afraid that even if you marry his son, he's not going to like you for a very long time. *(She puts a motherly arm around Jean)* But I do. And every chance I get, I'll sneak you into the kitchen and tell you so. *(She hugs Jean impulsively, as if they're saying goodbye)* Remember that. *(Turning to Buddy)* And you. I... oh, I love you, my sweet little boy.

> She buries her head on his shoulder.

BUDDY *(sheepishly)*: Thanks, Mom. Mom?

MRS. SINCLAIR: What, honey?

BUDDY: How are we going to get married? Nobody wants to marry us.

MRS. SINCLAIR *(sighs)*: Justice of the Peace, I guess.

JEAN: Oh, God.

BUDDY: What, honey?

JEAN: God, why is this so hard?

> Suddenly, the ENTIRE CREW rushes downstairs. CAPUTO is in labor.

CAPUTO: Oh, boy. This is it, kids!

CEIL: Fixie, go get a cab. *(He exits)* Marguerite—

MARGUERITE: I'm not going back into that kitchen!

CEIL: Go get Father Brendan.

CAPUTO *(scared)*: Why Father Brendan?

CEIL *(trying to look unconcerned)*: Just in case.

CAPUTO: In case of what?

CEIL *(changing the subject)*: Nicki, go call and leave word for Chick to meet us at the hospital when he gets back from fishing.

NICKI leaves. CEIL looks around.

Are we having a wedding? What's happening? Oh, hello, Mrs. Sinclair! *(Jumps back with sudden fear, looking around warily)* Is your husband back?

MRS. SINCLAIR: Oh, no. He's fast asleep.

There is a pounding at the door.

CEIL: Oh, thank God. Fixie's got a cab.

She opens the door. It's a furious MR. SINCLAIR.

MR. SINCLAIR: What in the goddamn hell is happening here? Sophie, you're really a pistol today, aren't you?

MRS. SINCLAIR: Ezra. I... you—

BUDDY: Dad, go home.

MR. SINCLAIR: Get over here.

BUDDY doesn't move.

Get over here.

> *BUDDY still doesn't move. There is a brief standoff. Then, MR. SINCLAIR lunges for Buddy. At first Buddy runs away and there's a burlesque chase around the living room furniture. Then, he recovers himself, and stands his ground. Mr. Sinclair, confused by the sudden change in strategy, stumbles. Then, he reaches for Buddy's hair. He gives it a good yank. Everyone gasps in sympathy pain. Mr. Sinclair looks triumphant.*

MR. SINCLAIR: Well? Are you coming home?

> *Glares in pure fury for a moment. Then, he begins to laugh— not unlike Jean, as it turns out.*

BUDDY: No! No!

Laughs merrily.

MR. SINCLAIR: He's' a lunatic, Sophie. He's over the edge.

> *JEAN starts laughing until the two lovers are helplessly holding each other, doubled over with laughter.*

She drove him to it. They're both nuts.

CAPUTO: I hate to interrupt, but I think my water just broke.

> *The door opens with MARGUERITE, pulling FATHER BRENDAN in.*

FATHER BRENDAN: The ships sailed without me. As I pulled up the last one in the fleet was pulling away from the dock.

MARGUERITE: You didn't get to bless them?

FATHER BRENDAN: Well, actually, I did, sort of. I lobbed a bottle of Holy water and smacked the last boat broadside. I think that counts. Am I too late?

CAPUTO *(between grimaces)*: Holy Joe won't marry them. Father, speaking of holy water, I wouldn't step right over there.

CEIL: Well, a lot has happened, Father. But we've got something more important for you. Angela is about to have a baby.

FATHER BRENDAN: About to have a baby?

CEIL: Yes, Father. I think she is.

FATHER BRENDAN: Are— can— we get her to a hospital?

CEIL: I don't know, Father. Her water just broke. *(Realizing)* Oh, my God! My mother's rug! *(Recovers herself)* I think you ought to stay here with her. Or go with her if we can get a taxi.

FATHER BRENDAN: A taxi! That's it! I'll get a taxi!

MARGUERITE: Fixie's out there now trying to get one.

BUDDY: I have my motorcycle.

MR. SINCLAIR: What is everybody standing around here for? Buddy, go get my Packard.

BUDDY *(sheepishly)*: It's up at the garage, Dad. Mom said we could borrow it for our honeymoon.

MR. SINCLAIR: Jesus Christ, Sophie!

> *CATHOLICS head-bow.*

What else have you done today? *(To Caputo)* Get upstairs. Wait there. *(Knowingly to Ceil)* You think that's best, do you, Miss O'Connell?

CEIL *(quietly)*: Yes.

MR. SINCLAIR: Buddy, you and this man help her upstairs.

FATHER BRENDAN: Oh, God.

MRS. SINCLAIR: I'll help.

> *The TWO MEN carry CAPUTO upstairs with MRS. SINCLAIR following.*

CEIL: Marguerite, now we really need that water. Come with me.

> *She and MARGUERITE go into the kitchen. Suddenly JEAN and MR. SINCLAIR are alone.*

JEAN: What should I do?

MR. SINCLAIR: Suit yourself.

JEAN: I guess you don't think I would be much help up there.

MR. SINCLAIR: Well, if you're gonna just laugh through the whole thing...

JEAN: Is my friend... in trouble?

MR. SINCLAIR: How should I know? You mean she's not married?

JEAN: No, no. She's married. I mean, is the baby alright?

MR. SINCLAIR: I'm just an old farm hick. But your cousin gave me a look. I don't know. And with everybody marching off to save the world, it's not so easy to get a cab in this city.

JEAN: Well, thank God Father Brendan's here.

MR. SINCLAIR: A lotta good that pantywaist'll do.

JEAN *(flaring)*: Hey! He's a nice guy!

MR. SINCLAIR: What do you think he's gonna do up there? Pray to a statue of Mary and make everything alright?

JEAN: I don't know.

MR. SINCLAIR: Well, I do. His being there ain't gonna matter one bit if that baby lives or dies.

JEAN: You— that's just awful!

MR. SINCLAIR: Whether it is or it isn't, he ain't no help.

JEAN: I think you're wrong. And not because I'm a Catholic. I think he's... well, he's there to make sure that God is watching over him. *(Realizing something)* That's all we want. Isn't it? To know that God's watching over us?

HOLY JOE comes into the house, followed by NICKI.

HOLY JOE: How is Angela? *(Sees Mr. Sinclair, pointedly ignores him)* Where is she?

JEAN: Upstairs, Father. Father Brendan's with her.

NICKI: I'm going up to see to her.

She exits upstairs.

HOLY JOE: I thought I told him to go to the shipyards.

JEAN: He did. He... missed the boat.

She giggles again.

HOLY JOE: I see you're taking this as seriously as you take your faith.

JEAN: Father— before you go upstairs, I have a confession to make.

HOLY JOE: You want to be married in a front parlor and now you want to make a confession there, too? Do you have any regard for the rules of the Church?

JEAN: No, Father, not that kind of confession. I mean, I want to admit something.

HOLY JOE: What?

JEAN: I... I'm not really a Catholic.

HOLY JOE: What?

JEAN: What I mean to say, Father, is, I don't really think I know what it means to be a Catholic. I thought it meant being... optimistic.

HOLY JOE: Optimistic?

JEAN: Yeah. Because no matter what you did, or who you were, you would see God and heaven one day.

HOLY JOE: Not if you die with sin on your soul, you won't.

JEAN: Well, that's the point. I just don't understand the fine print, as Buddy would say. I didn't get it. I thought if two people knew each other as well as we did, and obviously loved each other, that the church could see it. Because God can see it. *(Sighs)* So, until I can figure it out, I don't think I'm a Catholic. *(To Mr. Sinclair)* That oughta make you happy.

MR. SINCLAIR: Whether you want to be or not, you are. *(To Holy Joe)* Ain't that the way it is, you?

HOLY JOE *(for once, he is perplexed, finally, he speaks)*: I'd better see to Angela.

> We hear CAPUTO let out a rip-roaring "AGGGH! JESUS
> CHRIST!" from upstairs. HOLY JOE recoils, even if he and
> JEAN remember to bow their heads. BUDDY runs down the
> steps.

BUDDY: I'm not allowed up there any more.

> He stops cold at seeing HOLY JOE. Looks from him to his
> FATHER to JEAN.

What—? Honey, what's going on?

JEAN: I'm letting Monsignor know that I'm not a Catholic, I guess.

BUDDY: What?

JEAN: I thought we believed in forgiveness and helping people. Like African babies and refugees and lepers.

BUDDY: Honey, you don't have to—

JEAN: No. I just don't think I can be a Catholic anymore.

> She starts to cry. BUDDY holds her.

BUDDY *(to Holy Joe)*: Father, I'm ready to convert.

HOLY JOE, MR. SINCLAIR & JEAN: What?

BUDDY: She doesn't mean it. This whole thing just has her too upset. What do I need to do?

HOLY JOE: Well, there's a whole protocol. We just can't rush into anything.

MR. SINCLAIR: Walter Sinclair, you are not going over to their side.

> CEIL and MARGUERITE enter from the kitchen.

CEIL: I just called down the back alley to Mr. Zimmer the iceman. He'll take Angela to the hospital, if she can make it. *(Looking around)* Is anyone looking after Angela? *(No response)* There's a girl up there having her first baby. She should have it in a hospital, not in my bedroom!

CEIL (CONT'D): Father, you should be up there, not down here arguing. And you *(Meaning Mr. Sinclair)* should have been looking for a cab. For God's sake, stop flapping your gums and move!

FATHER BRENDAN runs down the steps.

FATHER BRENDAN: I really think we need to get to the hospital.

CEIL: Can you get her downstairs? I've got her a ride.

FATHER BRENDAN: Sure. Buddy, come give us a hand.

BUDDY bounds up the stairs, following FATHER BRENDAN.

MR. SINCLAIR *(somewhat subdued)*: What should I do?

CEIL: Give them your blessing. *(To Holy Joe)* You, too. But stop all this talking!

HOLY JOE: I am perfectly willing to—

CEIL: No, you're not! You want things your way! Well, don't we all. But if you've really been praying all these years, you know you don't always get what you want! This girl has seen both her parents die. She's had to make her own way, with the little bit of help her family could give her. She's had to put up with a spiteful selfish old guardian—

MARGUERITE: You shouldn't talk that way about Aunt Mary—

CEIL: —and you're getting just like her! And Buddy may very well have to go to war. What are you doing? Both of youse ought to be ashamed. Two wonderful young people just want to be happy. And they're both so confused, they want to give up the little bit of themselves that makes them who they are— to please two old men who don't even know what they want!

BUDDY and FATHER BRENDAN begin carefully carrying CAPUTO downstairs in a chair. MRS. SINCLAIR and NICKI follow. Caputo is obviously worn out, but the pain seems to have subsided.

CEIL: Oh, thank God. Out through the kitchen.

The BOYS head for the kitchen door.

CAPUTO *(weakly)*: Are you married yet?

JEAN starts to giggle.

Guess not. *(To Holy Joe)* Father?

HOLY JOE: Yes, Angela.

CAPUTO: C'mere for a second. *(He gingerly goes to her)* I just want to say...

She leans into his ear. A big labor pain.

Aaaauuugghhh!

HOLY JOE: She's possessed!

NICKI: She's having a baby, father.

CAPUTO: I just meant to ask you to please marry these kids, for God's sake. We Catholics haven't cornered the market on honesty. And Buddy's one of the nicest fellas I know.

JEAN *(very touched, goes to Caputo)*: Thanks, kid.

They hug.

CEIL: All of you, out! Mr. Zimmer's last load's melting halfway to water.

FATHER BRENDAN *(as he and Buddy run to the door)*: Monsignor, I humbly ask you to marry these two. If they ever break their word, I will assume the consequences— if there are any.

They exit.

MRS. SINCLAIR *(following them toward the kitchen, turns to Mr. Sinclair)*: Ezra? Waffles?

MR. SINCLAIR *(to Buddy)*: Where are you taking my Packard?

BUDDY: Ocean City, Sir.

MR. SINCLAIR *(reaches into his pocket, pulls out a money clip)*: Here's twenty bucks. If you go. If the deal gets queered, I want it back. *(To Ceil, quietly)* Miss O'Connell.

He and MRS. SINCLAIR leave.

CEIL: Father, I'll have these two down to the church in a half an hour. That is, unless you have some more ships to bless.

HOLY JOE: I'm not sure about all this.

CEIL: No one is sure of anything, father. You just have to... have faith. Right?

HOLY JOE: And the document?

BUDDY: No, Father.

HOLY JOE: Oh, very well. *(Looks at his watch)* Better make it noon. And it will have to be the rectory.

BUDDY looks at JEAN, questioningly.

JEAN: That's fine, Father.

HOLY JOE *(looks at Jinx at the landing)*: Genevieve, what are you doing in that?

JINX: I wanted to— oh, never mind.

She goes upstairs, pouting.

HOLY JOE: Noon, then.

He exits.

CEIL looks around the room.

CEIL: Well, I'd better get the ammonia out. That... stain... may have already set. *(Starts for kitchen, to herself)* What do you use to get out... whatever that is...

She exits.

BUDDY: Wow. It's going to happen, I guess.

JEAN *(smiles)*: Yep.

> *BUDDY takes her hand as he slips off his shoes. She follows suit. He leads up on the sofa. They slowly dance in each other's arms as the lights fade.*

CURTAIN

ABOUT STAGE RIGHTS

Based in Los Angeles and founded in 2000, Stage Rights is one of the foremost independent theatrical publishers in the United States, providing stage performance rights for a wide range of plays and musicals to theater companies, schools, and other producing organizations across the country and internationally. As a licensing agent, Stage Rights is committed to providing each producer the tools they need for financial and artistic success. Stage Rights is dedicated to the future of live theatre, offering special programs that champion new theatrical works.

To view all of our current plays and musicals, visit:

www.stagerights.com

Made in the USA
Lexington, KY
14 February 2017